Henri Rousseau

Carnival Evening (Un Soir de Carnival). *1886. Oil, 45 x 34¼ inches. Collection Louis E. Stern.*

Henri Rousseau

BY DANIEL CATTON RICH

"I have been told that my work is not of this century. As you will understand, I cannot now change my manner which I have acquired as the result of obstinate toil . . . . "
Henri Rousseau in a letter to the art critic, André Dupont, 1910.

IN COLLABORATION WITH THE ART INSTITUTE OF CHICAGO

THE MUSEUM OF MODERN ART, NEW YORK

Contents

Foreword

In 1939 when the Museum of Modern Art arranged the comprehensive exhibition Picasso: Forty Years of His Art, *the Art Institute of Chicago assisted the New York institution in various ways. So successful was this joint undertaking that further collaboration was planned. It was Chicago's turn next and had it not been for the war we would doubtless together have assembled another important one-man show before this. The impossibility of securing loans from Europe made us hesitate until it was discovered that in American collections alone were sufficient works by Henri Rousseau to present a comprehensive view of his art. Meanwhile another museum, the Albright Art Gallery of Buffalo, had contemplated such a showing but, with signal generosity, not only stepped aside but placed at our disposal such information as had already been brought together by the Director, Gordon Washburn.*

Paintings by Rousseau have been shown in many exhibitions at the Museum of Modern Art, particularly in 1938 when some of his works were included along with other "modern primitives" of Europe and America in Masters of Popular Painting. *In fact New York saw the first Rousseau exhibition as early as 1910, arranged shortly after his death by his friend, Max Weber, at "291," Alfred Stieglitz's gallery where so many important artists of the nineteenth and twentieth centuries have been introduced to America. Since that time many Rousseau canvases have entered our private and public collections, for aside from Germany, where he was quickly appreciated, no country, not even his own, has responded so warmly as the United States to his sincere and unassuming art.*

While the state of the world has prevented the loan of six or eight outstanding paintings from abroad, the exhibition here assembled not only illustrates the several sides of Rousseau's expression but contains a number of his most famous canvases. (This volume also includes a few reproductions of well-known paintings not in the exhibition.) The exhibition spans the period from 1886, the year of his first appearance in the Salon of the Independents, to his death in 1910. It is particularly strong in works done after 1900, doubtless because our collectors have found the exotic subjects of the master more to their taste than his portraits and allegories. Throughout, the object has been to show Rousseau not as a "naïve" eccentric but as an artist significant in his own right—one of the great painters of his generation.

This study of his life and work and in large part the exhibition are the work of the staff of the Art Institute of Chicago, but the Museum of Modern Art has lent its advice and support to the undertaking and has seen the present publication through the press.

ALFRED H. BARR, JR., Director, The Museum of Modern Art
DANIEL CATTON RICH, Director of Fine Arts, The Art Institute of Chicago

Acknowledgments

We wish to express appreciation to the following for the assistance which they rendered in assembling the exhibition: Mr. Gordon B. Washburn, director, and Dr. Heinrich Schwartz, of The Albright Art Gallery, Buffalo; Mr. John S. Newberry, curator of The Alger House Museum, Grosse Pointe Farms, Michigan; Mr. William M. Milliken, director, and Mr. Henry Sayles Francis, curator of paintings, of The Cleveland Museum of Art; Mr. Philip R. Adams, director of The Columbus Gallery of Fine Arts; Mr. Roland J. McKinney, director of The Los Angeles County Museum of History, Science and Art; Mr. Francis Henry Taylor, director, and Mr. Harry B. Wehle, curator of painting, of The Metropolitan Museum of Art, New York; Mr. Fiske Kimball, director, and Mr. Henri Marceau, assistant director, of The Philadelphia Museum of Art; Mr. Duncan Phillips, director of The Phillips Memorial Gallery, Washington, D. C.; Mr. Jere Abbott, director of The Smith College Museum of Art, Northampton, Massachusetts; Mrs. Murray Benton, supervisor of exhibits of The M. H. de Young Memorial Museum, San Francisco.

Mr. Paul Hyde Bonner, Rye Center, New Hampshire; Mr. Henry A. Botkin, New York; Mr. Stephan Bourgeois, New York; Mr. Joseph Brummer, New York; Mrs. Mary Bullard, New York; Mr. Carroll Carstairs, New York; Mrs. Emily Crane Chadbourne, Stone Ridge, New York; Mr. Leon Dabo, New York; Mrs. de Goldschmidt-Rothschild, New York; Mr. Valentine Dudensing, New York; Mrs. William Averell Harriman, New York; Mr. Dalzell Hatfield, Los Angeles; Miss Marie Hinkes, Chicago; Miss Selma Johnson, Chicago; Mr. Georges Keller, New York; Mr. Thomas Laughlin, Manhasset, L. I., New York; Miss Petronel Lukens, Chicago; Miss Louise Lutz, Chicago; Mr. Pierre Matisse, New York; Mr. J. B. Neumann, New York; Miss Dorothy Odenheimer, Chicago; Mr. Charles E. Olmstead, Assistant Professor, Department of Botany, of The University of Chicago; Mme. Hilla Rebay, New York; Mr. James N. Rosenberg, New York; Mr. Paul Rosenberg, New York; Miss Anne E. Sardi, New York; Mr. Louis E. Stern, New York; Mr. James Johnson Sweeney, New York; Mr. Robert H. Tannahill, Detroit; Mr. Curt Valentin, New York; Miss Margaret Wareing, Chicago; Mr. Max Weber, Great Neck, L. I., New York; Mr. Julius H. Weitz-ner, New York; Mr. Felix Wildenstein, New York; Miss Lelia Wittler, New York.

Chicago Public Library; Harvard College Library, Cambridge, Massachusetts; Library of Congress, Washington, D. C.; The Library of The Museum of Modern Art, New York; New York Public Library; Newberry Library, Chicago; Library of The State University of Iowa, Iowa City; Harper Memorial Library of The University of Chicago; The University of Illinois Library.

Lenders to the exhibition

The President and Trustees of The Art Institute of Chicago and of The Museum of Modern Art gratefully acknowledge the generous cooperation of the following lenders to the exhibition: Dr. and Mrs. Harry Bakwin, New York; Mr. and Mrs. Walter S. Brewster, Chicago; Mr. and Mrs. Henry Clifford, Radnor, Pennsylvania; Dr. and Mrs. Frank Conroy, New York; Chester Dale Collection, New York; Mr. Morton R. Goldsmith, Scarsdale, New York; Mrs. William Hale Harkness, New York; Mrs. Patrick C. Hill, Washington, D. C.; Mr. Sidney Janis, New York; Mr. and Mrs. Sam A. Lewisohn, New York; Dr. Franz Meyer, Zürich; Colonel Robert R. McCormick, Chicago; Mr. William S. Paley, Manhasset, L. I., New York; Mrs. John D. Rockefeller, Jr., New York; Mr. James Thrall Soby, Farmington, Connecticut; Mr. Louis E. Stern, New York; Mr. Max Weber, Great Neck, L. I., New York.

The Buffalo Fine Arts Academy, The Albright Art Gallery, Buffalo, New York; The Cleveland Museum of Art, Cleveland, Ohio; The Columbus Gallery of Fine Arts, The Ferdinand Howald Collection, Columbus, Ohio; The Solomon R. Guggenheim Foundation, New York; The Metropolitan Museum of Art, New York; The Philadelphia Museum of Art, Philadelphia; The Phillips Memorial Gallery, Washington, D. C.; The Smith College Museum of Art, Northampton, Massachusetts.

Mr. Jean Goriany, New York; The Marie Harriman Gallery, New York; Paul Rosenberg and Company, New York; Mr. Julius H. Weitzner, New York; Wildenstein and Company, Inc., New York.

Department of Painting and Sculpture: Alfred H. Barr, Jr., *Curator*; Dorothy C. Miller, *Associate Curator*.

Department of Architecture: Janet Henrich, *Acting Curator*.

Film Library: John E. Abbott, *Director*; Iris Barry, *Curator*; Edward F. Kerns, *Technical Director*; Allen Porter, *Circulation and Exhibition Director*.

Department of Industrial Design: Eliot F. Noyes, *Director*.

Department of Photography: Beaumont Newhall, *Curator*.

Department of Exhibitions: Monroe Wheeler, *Director*; Carlos Dyer, *Technical Assistant*.

Department of Circulating Exhibitions: Elodie Courter, *Director*.

Department of Publications: Monroe Wheeler, *Director*; Holger E. Hagen, *Manager*.

Library: Beaumont Newhall, *Librarian*.

Dance Archives: Paul Magriel, *Librarian*.

Publicity Department: Sarah Newmeyer, *Director*.

Department of Registration: Dorothy H. Dudley, *Registrar*.

Educational Project: Victor D'Amico, *Director*.

Information Desk: Ernest J. Tremp; Lillian Clark.

Key

Oil paintings are on canvas unless otherwise noted.

(Dated) following a date means that the date appears on the picture.

In dimensions, height precedes width.

Myself. Portrait-Landscape. 1890 (dated). Oil, 57½ x 44¾ inches. Collection The Modern Museum, Prague. Not in the exhibition.

Henri Rousseau

For half a century the art of Henri Rousseau has been obscured by an insistent and almost exclusive belief in its primitivism. Because the artist was self-taught and thereby lacked the studio training of his day, Rousseau was first scorned, then loved for his "naïveté." His enthusiasts allowed him no sources or development. He was simply a "primitive" (as the twentieth century conceived one) and automatically produced "marvelous" and "angelic" works in a vacuum. Though critics glorified the man (hundreds of stories exist to prove his ingenuousness), they tell little of his art. Three decades after Rousseau's death we lack the most significant details in his biography such as confirmation of his years in Mexico, details of his two marriages, and possible early associations with teachers and other artists; we are uncertain about the chronological order of his paintings and nowhere do we find a serious appraisal of his style.

Henri Julien Félix Rousseau was born in Laval, the chief town of the Department of Mayenne in northwestern France, on May 20, 1844. His family was poor, his father a humble dealer in tin ware (*ferblantier*), but his mother, Éléonore Guyard, seems to have descended from a family of some military prominence. Perhaps the chevaliers and colonels on her side of the house determined Henri to seek an army career. Though records are lacking, it is probable that in 1862, at the age of eighteen, he was sent to Mexico in the service of the ill-starred Emperor Maximilian as a musician in a military band. Returning to France in 1866, he was demobilized the next year and became a lawyer's clerk. Soon afterward he may have entered the customs service but in the War of 1870 he was back in the army with the rank of sergeant, saving (so he told afterwards) the town of Dreux "from the horrors of civil war." In 1871 he was given employment in a toll station on the outskirts of Paris, not as a customhouse officer (*douanier*) but as a minor inspector. All this time he had been compelled, as he says himself, "to follow a career quite different from that to which his artistic tastes invited him." Around 1885, when about forty, he retired on a tiny pension, determined to become known as a professional artist.

1880–1885

No painting dated before 1880 exists. But Rousseau had probably drawn and painted all his life. He was entirely self-taught, not because he scoffed at instruction (he later founded an "academy" and gave lessons) but because he had been too poor to enroll in an art school. The first little pictures that survive show him working in the amateur tradition of the 'eighties in France. Every self-taught painter starts under some pictorial influence. Rousseau began with memories of anonymous portraits, flower pieces, little romantic landscapes—the whole retarded idiom of folk painting which, especially since 1800, had been practiced all over Europe and the

13

New World. Regardless of period and quality such works bear a family resemblance.[1] Their forms are carefully adjusted to the surface of the painting and to the frame. The picture surface is developed geometrically, with an often inflexible rhythm of lines and spaces. The execution of details is minutely realistic. And because there usually lies at the bottom of such works the need to express a vital emotion, the result is full of expressive content. Figures with eyes gazing straight ahead are frozen in frontal pose. Perspective is centralized. Strong differences of proportion are stressed (tiny figures in a big landscape, an enormous figure against a dwarfed background) and severe contours surround areas of color, often without shadow or weight.

Rousseau's earliest work displays many of the same characteristics. These small formalized landscapes with water mills and bridges and these little portraits fit closely into the folk idiom. True, they have a lucidity of color, a delicate charm in their geometry which set them apart from the rank and file of amateur paintings, but had Rousseau stopped here he would have been only a forgotten figure in a minor tradition. Instead he chose to teach himself more. He now determined to observe the objective world about him with penetrating eyes and to seek counsel from above. As he himself expresses it, he "worked alone without any master but nature and some advice from Gérôme and Clément."

His choice of Gérôme is enlightening. In the 'eighties the painter of *The Last Prayer* and *The Two Majesties* was not only an idol of the Salon public, but a powerful professor in the École des Beaux-Arts, where one of his first acts had been an attempt to banish Manet. What he told Rousseau we have no way of knowing. The master always denounced hasty, careless sketches; he encouraged highly idealized and finished painting and at one time stated that the first merit of a canvas lay in its "luminous and alluring color." All this may have been delivered to the struggling painter over forty, just beginning so late in life his chosen career. Rousseau remarks that both Clément and Gérôme encouraged him in his "naïveté." Perhaps they were momentarily stirred out of themselves by a note of engaging freshness, or more likely they were trying to be kind to a man they considered hopeless.

Rousseau's struggle now becomes clear. He dreamed of becoming a great and successful painter but subconsciously he realized the limitations of the folk style. At the same time he stubbornly refused to relinquish its designed stability. His problem was to retain such elements as were intuitively necessary to his art and to transform them into a freer, more individual means of expression. That he was able to accomplish the first step in this solution is eloquently proved by *Carnival Evening* (frontispiece), exhibited in the newly created Salon of the Independents in 1886.

Fortunately for him the new Salon existed. In 1884 a group of painters, rebelling against the dead exclusiveness of the official Salon, organized a yearly showing without prizes or juries open to all artists. Odilon Redon was a vice-president and the Independents instantly became the battleground of Pointillism, the first movement to challenge Impressionism, which had been the radical movement of the 'seventies. In the very year that Rousseau made his debut

[1] MICHAILOW, NIKOLA. Zur begriffsbestimmung der laienmalerei. Zeitschrift für Kunstgeschichte 4 no5-6: 283–300 1935.

14

River Scene, Quai d'Auteuil. 1885 (dated). Ink on tan paper, 6½ x 4⅞ inches. Collection Max Weber.

Quai d'Auteuil. 1885 (dated). Ink on tan paper, 6 x 4½ inches. Collection Max Weber.

public indignation was running high against Signac, and Seurat's *Sunday Afternoon on the Island of La Grande Jatte* was the scandal of the exhibition.

1886–1891

In *Carnival Evening* the artist poses a problem to which he will return again and again. Two small figures in the foreground are designed against a screen of trees or foliage through which the eye is led, plane by plane, into deep, lighted space. What strikes us at once about this work of 1886 is Rousseau's extraordinary progress in the space of a few years. No longer is his vocabulary confined to a few handed-down forms. The delicate nerve-like branches of the trees are rendered with an authority which springs from a wider experience with nature. Only the sharpest observation could account for the shapes and tones of the cloud bands. And yet all that he takes from the objective world is fastidiously transformed and organized through a system of silhouette and clear light. Inventions of rhythm, correspondences of line abound. To make his vision more compelling, the artist gives every inch of his canvas the same scrupulous and sensitive execution. With a greater liberation of form comes a new sentiment. Rousseau intended *Carnival Evening* as a night poem and in the masquerading figures, the face at the

15

A Rendez-vous in the Forest. 1889. Oil, 36½ x 28¾ inches. Lent by The Marie Harriman Gallery.

window, the bare, towering trees and moonlit sky there first appears that note of strangeness so marked in all his imaginative painting.

In the two drawings (page 15) done a year before, Rousseau continues to analyze, with great delicacy, two motifs from nature. Before 1895 Rousseau admits that he made more than "200 drawings in pen and pencil," which must have played an important role in the formation of his style.

16

Medieval Castle (Le Château-Fort). *1889 (dated). Oil, 36½ x 38¾ inches. Lent by The Marie Harriman Gallery.*

A Rendez-vous in the Forest (page 16) is full of the same intense observation. The plan of *Carnival Evening* is reversed and the figures, instead of occupying the frontal plane, are seen through a complicated lattice of spring trees. Rousseau ornaments the lower half of the picture with the loving, detailed care of the folk-painter, but when it was finished and each leaf and twig had been woven into the pattern, he may have been dissatisfied with the result. In spite of its highly romantic theme—lovers in eighteenth-century costume meeting in the depths of

17

the forest—it yet lacked much he desired in a picture. And so in its companion, a night piece, *Medieval Castle* (page 17), he boldly designs in larger forms of dark and light, restricting surface elaboration to a few passages in the trees. In place of filigreed planes appears a striking diagonal arrangement of flat areas.

Meanwhile the artist was living with his second wife in the most humble surroundings of the Plaisance quarter in Paris. He did all sorts of small jobs to eke out his pension, such as serving as inspector of sales for a newspaper, writing letters and acting as legal adviser to the poor of the district. His wife opened a little stationery shop where his pictures were always on sale and he painted a certain number of portraits of his neighbors. For a time he taught drawing in a municipal school and was made *Officier de l'Instruction Publique*, wearing the violet button which he proudly displays in his self-portrait of 1890 (page 12). This is a "portrait-landscape," a genre familiar in his work. The model is fitted out with a background appropriate in both sentiment and design. For himself he chose the festive Paris of the *Exposition Universelle* of 1889, complete with Eiffel Tower and balloon. He stands—a much taller figure than in life—holding brush and a palette inscribed with "Clémence" and "Joséphine," the names of his two wives. Clearly this is his strongly held vision of himself, a respectable "professor of art" determined to become one of the great painters of his age.

At first the age denied him. Not that his pictures were ignored even when skyed or tucked away in the coldest corners of the Independents where, between the years 1886 and 1890, he showed twenty works. The public found them out and laughed uproariously. Critics poked fun at him. Rousseau did not falter. Industriously he collected his press notices and pasted them into a book. Next to one he noted: "Wrote to the journalist for his insulting article. Made excuses."

But if the public was amused and critics misunderstood, a few artists took a second look at these paintings, which seemed so opposed in style and feeling to the main currents of their day. The decade of the 'eighties saw the start of a major shift in artistic ideals. With the rejection or disciplining of Impressionism interest in the illusion of nature began to slacken. Painters turned back to a more permanent structure, seeking in archaic styles of the past a new way to organize the data of vision. Puvis de Chavannes had feebly indicated one approach. Seurat devised a method to bring order into Impressionism, joining to it the tradition of classical design. And Gauguin went back to the primitive. So it is not surprising to discover Gauguin admiring Rousseau for his "blacks" at a time when black had been fashionably banished from the palette. And about 1888 Odilon Redon and Gustave Coquiot, defender of the Independents, began, according to the latter, "to celebrate Rousseau's genius as a naturalist painter who sometimes attained a beautiful classic style."

Seurat, meanwhile, had sought to energize his stable forms with movement (*Le Chahut*, 1889–90, *The Circus*, 1891); Degas was working with larger rhythms and Toulouse-Lautrec was constantly increasing the activity and flow of his line. All that Rousseau had painted so far was static, fixed and immobile. Such movement as existed came through rhythmic repeat of small elements rather than through any big, inclusive design. But in 1891 he labored hard

Storm in the Jungle. 1891 (dated). Oil, 50½ x 63½ inches. Collection Mr. and Mrs. Henry Clifford.

over a large picture, *Storm in the Jungle* (above). It represents the height of his romanticism and the first use of exotic material. Here he subdued his delight in elaboration of detail to a more general movement of the forms. All is still conceived in planes but the artist now twists and entwines them. Light not only defines but contributes atmosphere to the dramatic theme. The complex color, with contrasts of browns, greens and red, results in part from the artist's almost literal rendering of plant forms. His chief concession to surface lies in striping the entire canvas with lines of thin rain.

Friends of Rousseau once explained his jungle pictures as memories of his Mexican journey. But today we know they were inspired by trips to the Paris zoo and botanical gardens. In a vaudeville sketch written about this time and entitled *A Visit to the Exposition of 1889* (page 76) one of the ten scenes is significantly set in the *Jardin des Plantes*. On his walks round Paris the artist used to pick up leaves and grasses to treasure in his studio. From such sources—transfigured by imagination and design—grew his exotic flora.

Pont de Grenelle, Paris. 1891–93. Oil, 8 x 29¾ inches. Private Collection.

1892–1897

During the next few years Rousseau strives constantly to broaden and simplify his style. In such a canvas as *Pont de Grenelle* (above) he sternly limits the number of planes and reduces the color to a few tones. Against the stark areas of snow and the stone bridge, the shapes of figures and lumber-cart are silhouetted with extraordinary force. With complete freedom he combines various perspectives and adjusts space to fill the long, narrow format. Unlike the Impressionists, who preferred the colorful and gay life along the river at La Grenouillère, Chatou or Bougival, Rousseau seldom went far from home for his landscape motifs. He loved the heart of the city with its iron bridges, boats and quais or the quiet suburbs where, as in *Sawmill, Outskirts of Paris* (page 21), he enjoyed painting factory buildings surrounded by trees and foliage. By this time Rousseau is learning not only to bind his forms more strongly into a single geometric unit but to vary his textures. His technique has the same fineness of touch but the touch itself is less uniform or labored.

Color so far had been distinctly subordinate to tone and draughtsmanship. The night pieces of the 'eighties and the detailed color of *Storm in the Jungle* do not prepare us for the bright hues and luminous atmosphere of *The Carmagnole* (below). To the Salon of the Independents in 1892 the artist sent as his exhibition piece a large canvas, *The Centenary of Independence*. *The Carmagnole* is perhaps the first sketch for the big painting. For Rousseau the centenary

The Carmagnole. 1891–92. Oil, 7½ x 30 inches. Collection Dr. and Mrs. Frank Conroy.

20

Sawmill, Outskirts of Paris. 1893–95 (?). Oil, 10 x 18 inches. Collection Mr. and Mrs. Walter S. Brewster.

was a genuinely inspiring event. He wrote an explanation for the catalog: "The people, holding hands, dance round the two Republics, those of 1792 and 1892, to the tune of *Auprès de ma blonde qu'il fait bon, fait bon dormir.*" A year later he addressed a second picture to Liberty ("Oh, Liberty, be forever the guide of those who by their labor wish to contribute to the glory and grandeur of France!"). Such sentiments show Rousseau's genuine and simple love of his country but they also indicate his firm belief that as one of the most important artists of the day he must commemorate for the citizens of France the anniversary of their Republic.

Behind the composition may lie a suggestion of some *kermess* by Bruegel or Teniers, but the spirit is gaily French. Notes of color are repeated in the circling figures and in the fluttering banners (all arranged to blow in the same direction), while space is clearly marked off by the reiterated vertical of the flagpoles. When Rousseau came to paint the final version, he changed the format and completely re-designed the whole picture—an indication of how much he continued to respect the relation of a painting to its surface and frame.

But if the artist hoped to win public acclaim by such patriotic subjects he was doomed to disappointment. Indeed, there was even talk on the part of some of the more arbitrary members of the Committee of the Independents of banishing altogether those artists whose work brought nothing but laughter in the annual Salon. Fortunately tolerance won, the painter of *The Carmagnole* being well defended by Toulouse-Lautrec. It is said that Rousseau was in favor of the exclusion, never dreaming for a moment that it was aimed at him.

The still life, *Poet's Bouquet* (page 23), carries on his interest in color and more simplified

21

handling. The background, table top and vase are broadly painted to allow an enriched concentration on the flowers themselves. Not only does he award each blossom and leaf the same prominence, but he tries to communicate the growing sensitive life of flowers even after they are plucked. The ones on the left are significantly set against a blue ground suggesting the sky. Though there are relatively few flowers, Rousseau manages to convey the sense of a complete garden. This ability to make a small, intensely rendered part stand for the whole is characteristic of his vision. Rousseau's power of abbreviation constantly advances as he strives for larger expression.

The sentiment of flowers was strong in him. Later in 1908 when he was painting the portrait of Guillaume Apollinaire and Marie Laurencin (*The Muse Inspiring the Poet*) he instructed his friend to purchase *l'œillet de poète* (sweet william) and when gilliflowers (*giroflées*) turned up instead and got themselves painted into the picture, he insisted on doing a second version with the correct flowers in place.

By 1895 Rousseau was known to many leading artists. Through constant exhibition in the Independents (where every year he trundled his canvases to the Salon in a little cart) he had slowly won the interest of a new generation beginning to be concerned with invented rather than observed forms. As early as 1890 Maurice Denis had written: "Remember that a picture—before it is a war horse, a nude woman or an anecdote—is essentially a plane surface covered with colors arranged in a certain order." Among others Paul Sérusier and Charles Guérin made his acquaintance and in 1893 he was introduced to Degas at the Gauguin exhibition. According to Vollard, Degas, on another occasion, bored by the many new theories expounded at the Independents, suddenly turned round and pointed at a picture. "Why shouldn't that be the painter of the future?" It was a work by Rousseau. When a prominent art critic was preparing a volume on the leading artists of the day, Rousseau appeared at the publisher's with his own biographical sketch along with a self-portrait drawn in ink. The account is full of interest. He suppresses all details of his early life save the place of his birth, his birth date and early poverty. No mention is made of a military career, the voyage to Mexico or the long years in the customs. "It is only after great hardships and struggles that he has succeeded in making himself known to the numerous artists who now surround him," Rousseau wrote. "He has perfected himself more and more in the original manner which he adopted and he is in process of becoming one of our best realist painters. As a characteristic mark he wears a bushy beard (*la barbe broussaillante*). He has been a member of the Independents for many years, believing that complete freedom of production should be given to any initiator whose mind aspires to the Beautiful and the Good."[1]

Such simplicity tempted tricks. Friends convinced him that the President of the Republic had invited him to dinner. On another occasion a man dressed as Puvis de Chavannes (then a great figure in the Paris art world) visited the humble studio. "I have been waiting for you a long time," remarked Rousseau as he graciously showed the impostor his recent canvases.

[1] First published by Soupault (bibl. 50) and in Wilenski (bibl. 63) from which the present translation comes.

Poet's Bouquet (Fleurs de poète). 1890–95. Oil, 15 x 18 inches. Collection William S. Paley.

The Horrors of War. 1895. Lithograph on red paper, 8½ x 12½ inches. (Reproduced as the end sheets of this catalog.) Lent by Jean Goriany.

In the 'nineties Rousseau also met Alfred Jarry, the Bohemian author of *Ubu-Roi*. They were both natives of Laval, where Rousseau had known Jarry's father. The meeting is said to have taken place at the Independents, where Rousseau was standing beside his pictures. Instantly impressed by their strangeness, Jarry commissioned a portrait. Complete with parrot and chameleon the picture made its appearance in the Independents of 1894. (As early as 1891 Rousseau had exhibited a portrait of Pierre Loti with a cat, but since there is no record that he knew Loti, the picture may have been done from a photograph or newspaper cut.)

Through Jarry, Rousseau was introduced to Rémy de Gourmont who ordered a lithograph for the magazine, *L'Imagier*. This—his only print—is connected with a canvas of *War* (since lost) shown in 1894. For the catalog Rousseau wrote the following legend: "Frightful, she passes, leaving in her wake, despair, tears and ruin." Though once a soldier, Rousseau hated war. "If a King wants to wage war let a mother go to him and forbid it," he often remarked.

This lithograph, with its strongly Expressionist tendencies, continues the sense of movement first attempted in *Storm in the Jungle* (page 19).

At times this desire for movement within the canvas is abandoned for an intensified striving toward the monumental. The severely frontal *Portrait of a Young Girl* (page 26) shows him

25

Portrait of a Young Girl. 1893–95. Oil, 24 x 18 inches. Collection Philadelphia Museum of Art.

seeking to bind figure and landscape into firmer union. The straight up and down pose is repeated again and again in the tree trunks, giving the composition a primitive verticality. Undoubtedly the model belonged to the *petit bourgeois* circles of the Plaisance quarter but as was his custom in portraits he devised a special out-of-door setting. There is something touching in Rousseau's struggle to surround this maiden with the symbols of pastoralism. The sheep at her feet, the trees in young leaf, the distant, lighted sky are painted with the same exactitude as the yellow boots and impassive face. At about this period the artist exhibited several portraits of children in the Independents. *Boy on Rocks* (page 27) may be one of them. Rousseau had a particular fondness for children, whom he portrayed in all their dignity and intensity.

26

Boy on Rocks. 1895–97. Oil, 21½ x 17¾ inches. Lent by The Chester Dale Collection.

Undoubtedly he was influenced by the cabinet photograph, but nothing is less photographic than the result. The artist's increasing interest in a few clear forms turns the velvet suit, striped dress, and stockings into a striking pattern. The "Alpine" landscape repeating the lines of the figure may derive from the fortifications around Paris. In another portrait such "rocks" were so explained by Rousseau.

In a series of landscapes Rousseau now attempts to paint with a broader touch. One of his heritages from the folk tradition was the linear marking-off of a canvas. Strong lines divide the surface into areas to be filled with color, almost in the manner of a mosaic. But the more he probed nature and came in contact with other paintings, the more Rousseau realized that too

27

Footbridge at Passy (La Passerelle de Passy). *1895. Oil, 17½ x 20 inches. Collection Morton R. Goldsmith.*

much of the linear, like too much ornamentation, may reduce the force of a picture. Unconsciously, perhaps, he was working towards that sustained unity found in the background of *The Sleeping Gypsy* of 1897 (page 33).

In some of his views of the Parc Montsouris done about this time, he strives for a more painter-like approach. Instead of defining each leaf he indicates a tree as a mass, then builds up its modeling with a broad stroke or stipple. Edges tend to lose their crispness, and a generalized shape replaces the once complicated detail.

Unconsciously but definitely Rousseau begins to obtain more feeling of depth. Painting in superimposed flat planes remained always his favorite way of composing but at this period he explores various devices of perspective. The tilting plane of the river in *Footbridge at Passy* (above) adds a dimension that many of his early landscapes lacked. He avoids exact balance, learning better how to echo a dark mass with a light or to return movement with counter-movement. Broader zones of color are made to answer their complements.

28

Artillerymen. c. 1895. Oil, 32 x 39½ inches. Collection The Solomon R. Guggenheim Foundation.

Artillerymen (above) belongs with the lost canvases of *War* (exhibited 1894) and *The Last of the 51st* (exhibited 1893) to that brief period when Rousseau turned towards military themes. One suspects a group photograph as the basis for the picture. But the set arrangement of the soldiers and the stressed darks and lights are employed by Rousseau with a wholly fresh insight. The landscape, as usual, is carefully keyed to the pattern of figures.

All the knowledge that Rousseau had added to his natural gift, all the freedoms he had gained by ten years of intense labor are incorporated into his greatest painting of the 'nineties, *The Sleeping Gypsy* (page 33), exhibited at the Independents in 1897. For such works "he had perfected himself more and more in the original manner which he adopted" and such a picture was intended to prove him "one of our best realist painters."

Realism is not the first quality one attributes to *The Sleeping Gypsy*. But its painter consciously meant it to be a naturalistic work. Here, I believe, he tried to rival his mentor, Gérôme, famous for African subjects with wild animals portrayed in bare stretches of landscape.

29

Gérôme's canvas, *The Caravan*, shows a tiger watching the advance of a desert party from his lonely promontory, and *The Two Majesties* depicts a lion (curiously like the beast in Rousseau's canvas) gazing at the setting sun which casts its clear orange beams across a deserted, sandy waste.

We know Rousseau's respect for meticulous painting of this sort. He greatly admired Bouguereau and Courtois, pointing out to amused friends their perfection of finish. But labor as he might to equal their effects, *The Sleeping Gypsy* is not another Salon machine. Unconsciously Rousseau created the subject in his own manner, making use of Gérôme's material as he made use of nature, not to copy its detail but to recast and reconstruct its elements.

In place of Gérôme's skilled description Rousseau gives us a vision expressed in purely plastic terms. As in *Carnival Evening* (frontispiece), painted eleven years before, it is the artist's organizing imagination at work which lends the picture its power. But where the earlier painting stressed the lyricism of night and masquerade, this canvas instantly sets up an uncanny, dream-like mood. The delicate forms of Rousseau's style of the 'eighties are replaced by forms of such grandeur that inevitably one compares them to some French classic master of the past. Here the enrichment of surface is limited to a few areas like the striped robe of the gypsy and the lion's mane. The fixed, dramatic tension between animal and figure is heightened by the play of large planes set in vast space; the harmony of color, reinforced by the moonlight, binding the forms together in a highly abstract way. Finally, it is the indissoluble union of design and poetry that makes *The Sleeping Gypsy* one of the strangest and most moving paintings in all of modern art.

Rousseau himself thought so well of the picture that he offered the canvas to his birthplace for a few hundred francs. Presumably it was sent to Laval but never hung. (It would be interesting to imagine its reception in this provincial French town at the end of the last century.) But though Laval rejected it, the painting was to become a forerunner of several twentieth-century developments. The motif of mandolin and vase (see detail, page 32) suggests later still lifes by Picasso and Braque. Its trance-like character foretells Surrealism and was especially influential when in 1926, after long years of disappearance, the picture was shown in an exhibition of the John Quinn collection in Paris. Jean Cocteau celebrated its rediscovery in a typical prose-poem in which he suggests that the lion and the landscape are a projection of the gypsy's dream and not thought of as actually present—an interpretation which seems more characteristic of the Surrealism of the moment than the method of Rousseau in 1897. Wilenski notes that de Chirico's *Lion and Gladiators* (1927, Detroit Institute of Arts) stems directly from it.

The *Tiger Hunt* (page 31), perhaps earlier than 1897, reflects the same interest in the North African themes of Fromentin and Gérôme. Such works were painted in Rousseau's small studio at 2 *bis*, rue Perrel, where he occupied a room over a plasterer's shop. His second wife had died and there he lived alone, composing his poems and dramas (page 76) and founding a "Philo-technical Association" to teach all the arts. Since his youth he had played the flute, mandolin and cornet and performed so adequately on the violin that he was hired for concerts in the

Tiger Hunt. 1895–97. Oil, 15 x 18⅛ inches. Collection The Columbus Gallery of Fine Arts. Ferdinand Howald Collection.

Tuileries Gardens. His prospectus advertises courses in music, diction, painting and drawing for children and adults. On Thursday evenings he conducted a sketch class from the model. The fee was eight francs a month, later raised to ten. He occasionally received commissions for portraits, even trading pictures to his baker or grocer.

1898–1906

The Sleeping Gypsy marks a turning point in Rousseau's career. In it he finally joined the geometry of the folk style to his own freer conventions of drawing and color. The expressional content of folk painting has been merged into an individual expression. Starting with a limited repertory of visual symbols, the artist, with infinite patience and intuitive understanding, has finally developed his personal language. From now on there is no longer that sign of struggle

31

Mandolin and Vase, detail from The Sleeping Gypsy. *This section of the canvas points forward to certain Cubist still lifes by Picasso and Braque.*

The Sleeping Gypsy. 1897 (dated). Oil. 51 x 70 inches. Collection The Museum of Modern Art, New York. Gift of Mrs. Simon Guggenheim.

Landscape, Outskirts of Paris (Paysage de Banlieue, Environs de Paris). *1898–1900. Oil, 15 x 18 inches. Collection The Cleveland Museum of Art.*

with architectonics or poetry, often found in preceding works. Rousseau moves easily in the world of his creation, *realizing* (in the sense that Cézanne used the word) as easily and clearly as he imagines.

   With a few notable exceptions this period is one of resting. After the intense effort of carrying through a few large paintings, Rousseau turns to smaller things. To the Independents he sends chiefly little landscapes and portraits. The landscapes are apt to include in their titles the time of year (*View of the Bois de Boulogne* [*autumn*]) or refer to some effect of light (*Lake Dumesnil* [*setting sun*]). The best of them, like the *Landscape, Outskirts of Paris* (above), contain clear blue skies, fluttering clouds, green trees, rose and red and gray houses, but though Rousseau remains faithful to local colors, there is an atmospheric envelopment very different from the earlier concentration on a few flat tones and severe boundaries. If, in their muted harmonies

Street Scene (sketch for View of Malakoff). *1898. Oil, 7½ x 11¼ inches. Collection Max Weber.*

and fineness of feeling, such landscapes at times recall Corot just back from his first Italian trip, on other occasions their perfection of hue and cool light remind us of the early Sisley and Pissarro. But beneath softer contours and freer brushwork still lies Rousseau's sense of completeness.

From about this time come his first painted sketches from nature. Like his drawings these preliminary studies before the motif have not been popular with critics seeking to celebrate Rousseau as an inspired "primitive." As a matter of fact, from the first Rousseau had been curiously dependent upon the object. Now he began to make on the spot, quick, summary sketches which he would later take back to the studio and rework into finished landscapes.

These sketches show a new side of Rousseau's abilities, since they are painted in a deft, Impressionist technique, with hazy, soft edges, dusky shadows and trembling lights. He did not think of them as pictures but as indications for pictures. He never approved of highly finished sketches or sketchy paintings. They show that had he wished, he might have excelled as an Impressionist. There is a charm in their green or gray tone, and a special sensitivity in their casual effects of light. The handling is easy and spontaneous, showing how remarkable was the artist's first response to nature.

36

View of Malakoff. 1898 (dated). Oil, 18 x 21¾ inches. Collection A. Villard, Paris. Not in the exhibition.

In his studio Rousseau would compose his landscape somewhat on the basis of the sketch. Where everything appeared blurred or softly brushed together, he would clarify and separate. This method has been compared to Seurat's but the likeness is superficial. Seurat's little sketches before nature were fragments of experience, analyzed according to a highly scientific theory of color contrasts and comparisons. Rousseau's were rapid, total impressions, made to fix the main shapes and color areas of the motif. Where Seurat eventually wove dozens of such little *croquetons* into one magisterial composition, Rousseau let these brief records stand for nature in the studio. How drastically he made them over may be seen by comparing a sketch (page 36) with the completed landscape (above).

In 1899 and 1900 Rousseau did not exhibit in the Salon of the Independents, but in 1901 he showed what is presumably the composition of a nude maiden, bear and hunter, entitled *An*

Unpleasant Surprise (Mauvaise surprise) (Barnes Foundation, Merion, Pa.).[1] It carries on the monumental dream qualities of *The Sleeping Gypsy* and elicited, according to Vollard, considerable admiration from Renoir. "What a beautiful tone in that picture by Rousseau," the painter remarked, "and the female nude . . . I'm sure that even Ingres wouldn't have disliked that!" The mention of Ingres in connection with growing appreciation of Rousseau comes at a time when the early nineteenth-century classical masters, long despised, were being rehabilitated. In 1902 Maurice Denis published his famous essay on the pupils of Ingres, calling attention to Ingres' early enthusiasm for Italian primitives at Assisi and Perugia, and stressing his artistic doctrine, which recognized the role of naïveté. In opposition to such reborn classicism there was everywhere a growing interest in exoticism and the exotic arts, one manifestation of which can be found in the emergence of the *Fauves*. Rousseau in 1904 sent to the Independents his *Scouts Attacked by a Tiger* (Barnes Foundation, Merion, Pa.), probably the first of his tropical compositions since *Storm in the Jungle* of 1891. (The same tiger appears in both.) And at about this period he painted the two small jungle scenes (pages 40 and 41), so close in size and complementary in mood that he perhaps intended them as a pair.

The contrast with Rousseau's early use of such material is significant. In place of detailed forms sharp with drawing, we find sensitively painted silhouettes crisscrossing and overlapping against the light. Gone are the frenzy of mood and the movement of planes. All is quiet, mysterious and poised. The hours of twilight and moonlight, with great beasts half hidden in the jungle, provide an opportunity for him to express that fantasy which, especially since *The Sleeping Gypsy*, had been a commanding element in everything he did.

The enormous and mural-like painting, *The Hungry Lion . . .*, shown at the new Autumn Salon of 1905, suddenly focused attention upon the painter. This was the famous Salon of the *Fauves*. A gallery was set aside for their work and one critic, Louis Vauxcelles, christened it "a cage of wild beasts," a better description of Rousseau's own entry a few rooms away. By being shown not in an enormous and indiscriminate exhibit but in the company of Manet, Toulouse-Lautrec and Redon, and along with the revolutionary young *Fauves*, Rousseau finally seemed to relate to the experimental movements of the nineteenth and twentieth centuries rather than to an eccentric and old-fashioned idiom. Myopic critics might still pronounce his work "ridiculous," but young painters like Delaunay, Vlaminck, Marie Laurencin and Picasso, and writers like Guillaume Apollinaire and André Salmon began to be fascinated with the man as well as his art.

In Rousseau's personality this generation pretended to discover all the virtues of the "primitive soul" which Gauguin had traveled so far to find, and best of all these virtues could be experienced here in Paris, no farther away than the rue Perrel. They remembered that in forming his own style Gauguin had consulted the *images d'Épinal*, and they began to seek out the work of the self-taught and to extol it.

This sudden interest in Rousseau was part of a wider return to historic sources, which characterizes so much of the advanced artistic experiment of our century. His impeccable technique led them back to French and Italian primitives while his intuitive inventions helped to justify

[1] Usually dated 1891.

Owl. c. 1905. Oil on wood, 9¾ x 6
inches. Collection Paul Petit, Paris.

Bird of Prey, detail of The Hungry Lion . . .
Collection Dr. Franz Meyer, Zürich.

(Comparison from Egger, bibl. 19.)

their own conscious experiment. At first they treated him with a half-loving condescension. Max Weber recalls Rousseau's appearance at the elder Madame Delaunay's salon, a small, modest figure, with a sweet piping voice and the simplicity of a child. This was the man who represented in the flesh what the young sophisticates had named *le style concierge*.

Aside from establishing his reputation and marking the theme which was to engross Rousseau for the last five years of his life, *The Hungry Lion* . . . has a deeper interest, for it furnishes another clue to his method. A sketch of an owl (evidently made from life) has survived (above) which Rousseau later made over into a bird of prey and set among the leaves of his great composition (detail, above). It is instructive to follow the subtle changes in design and feeling by which this transformation took place.

In later landscapes the note of fantasy, ever stronger, expresses itself in a freer association of forms and in richer implications of color and texture. In addition *Banks of the Oise* (page 42) and *House, Outskirts of Paris* (page 44) possess the dream-like serenity of some of the jungle compositions. (A preliminary sketch from nature for the latter picture belongs to Professor E. R. Weiss of Berlin.) The vibrant stippling of the trees in *Landscape, Pontoise* (page 45) reminds one of the dotted touch of the Pointillists, without their broken color. Perhaps Rousseau responded, unconsciously, to some such influence, but he put it to far different use. He was still strongly moved to objectify, having such unyielding respect for every object in nature that he wished to convey the sense of each leaf, if only by the briefest indication. Such late land-

Jungle with a Lion. 1904–06. Oil, 14¾ x 18 inches. Collection The Museum of Modern Art, New York. The Lillie P. Bliss Collection.

40

The Jungle: Lion and Buffalo. 1904–06. Oil, 14¾ x 17½ inches. Collection Mr. and Mrs. Sam A. Lewisohn.

41

Banks of the Oise. 1905. 18 x 22 inches. Collection The Smith College Museum of Art.

42

The Goatherd. 1905–07 (?). Oil, 16¼ x 21¼ inches. Collection James Thrall Soby.

43

House, Outskirts of Paris. 1905–07. Oil 13¾ x 18¼ inches. Collection Max Weber.

scapes, lit with romantic light and exquisite in color, contrast markedly with the spare and geometricized city views of the 'nineties. *Banks of the Oise*, moreover, contains a curious telescoping of several motifs, combined into an imaginative unity which leads directly on to the artist's last phase.

1907–1910

Now commenced the fullest period of Rousseau's life. His dream had come true. At the age of sixty-three he found himself in the center of the most advanced group of artists and writers in Paris, admired and recognized by the intellectual world. In 1907 he received his first large commission from Madame Delaunay for the *Snake-Charmer*, now in the Louvre. Its exhibition in the Autumn Salon brought him wide fame. But nothing turned his head. He still remained the ingenuous "artist-painter," accepting applause with the same tranquillity with which he had met abuse. Though he had acquired a dealer, Joseph Brummer, who was able to sell a few works for him now and then for small sums, he remained poor all his life, hardly knowing (as his

Landscape, Pontoise. 1906 (dated). Oil, 15½ x 12½ inches. Collection Mrs. William Hale Harkness.

Henri Rousseau. From a photograph owned by Max Weber. Inscribed: "Gift to my friend Weber artist-painter. Paris 14/12, 1903. Henri Rousseau artist-painter."

letters prove) where his next meal was coming from. "Having my rent to pay, then a big bill at my color merchant's, I am very short of money and this evening I have only 15 centimes for supper." (Letter to Guillaume Apollinaire, April 28, 1909.)

Max Weber, who as an art student in Paris at the time knew him intimately, has described his studio. Rousseau lived in a single room with a large window. There he painted, slept and did his modest cooking. On the walls was a plaster cast of an Egyptian relief (for him all supreme art was "Egyptian," including the paintings of Gauguin and Picasso) and over his cot hung *Present and Past*, a curious double portrait of himself and his second wife. A hideous statue on a pedestal, his violin, a few chairs and a red sofa, soon to be immortalized in the canvas, *The Dream* (page 68), made up the other furnishings. All about him were pictures, and when a visitor from the great world asked if it was not uncomfortable to sleep in a studio he replied, "You know, when I wake up I can smile at my canvases."

There he painted in a trance-like stillness from morning to night, slowly proceeding from the top to the bottom of his canvas. A picture might take two or three months and he was in luck if he received a hundred francs for it. Sometimes, Apollinaire relates, when he was engaged in a fantastic subject, he was overcome with fear and rushed trembling to open a window. On another occasion he told his biographer, Wilhelm Uhde, that his hand was being guided by the

46

spirit of his departed wife. When Uhde met Rousseau for the first time, the *Snake-Charmer* was on his easel. "I realized already that the legend of his artistic 'naïveté' was unjustified. He was concerned with the general harmony and balance of the large composition and asked my advice whether to make a tone darker or lighter, whether to suppress something here or add something there."

Occasionally Rousseau visited the Louvre and discussed the paintings afterward with nice understanding. "Which ones did you like best?" he was asked. "You see there are so many of them I forget the names," Rousseau replied. Brummer recalls that he mentioned only Courbet with admiration. (*Boat by a Cliff*, formerly in the collection of Paul Guillaume, Paris, seems to recall Courbet.) He conscientiously attended the official Salon where he led his pupils before the most academic examples. To the end of his life Bouguereau remained his idol and Bouguereau's death is said to have affected him deeply. At the Cézanne Memorial of 1907 his comment was, "You know, I could finish all these pictures."

The artist loved festivity and during the years 1908 and 1909 organized a series of musical soirées in his studio. Special invitations were sent out and a hand-decorated program given to each guest. Several descriptions of these events have appeared in print, of which the most precise is Adolph Basler's (translated from bibl. 8):

It was with Max Weber that I sometimes went to the soirées in the rue Perrel. This American, a tenor who apparently had sung in synagogues, was the chief soloist of these friendly affairs where

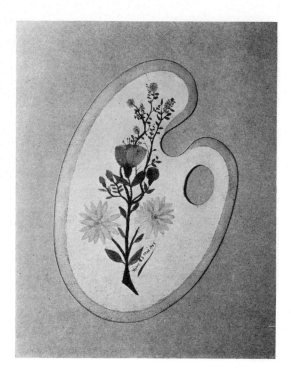

Rousseau's Palette. 1907 (dated). Wood, 8⅛ x 6⅛ inches. Collection Mrs. John D. Rockefeller, Jr.

Merry Jesters (Joyeux Farceurs). *1906. Oil, 57 x 44 inches. Collection Mr. and Mrs. Walter Conrad Arensberg.* Not in the exhibition.

48

The Jungle: Tiger Attacking a Buffalo. 1908 (dated). Oil, 67½ x 75 inches. Lent by Mrs. Patrick C. Hill to the Joseph Winterbotham Collection of The Art Institute of Chicago.

artists elbowed the people of the neighborhood. I noticed, among the guests, the baker with his daughter who was taking mandolin lessons from the Douanier, the little grocer round the corner, flanked by his son to whom Rousseau taught violin and drawing; the daughters of the milkman, some small business-men, a few retired inspectors from the customs and even the old eccentrics who passed their days painting by the side of their good-natured Patron. An old architect's clerk, the most persistent habitué of the place, boasted of representing the intellectual element. He teased the poor Douanier and his humble public continually. But he was the one who started the stupidest songs of the evening, particularly one threadbare old piece of the Second Empire in which all the company joined in the chorus: "Ah, Ah, Joséphine . . ."

49

This concert, not in the least symphonic, always began with the Marseillaise. Henri Rousseau, first violin, directed the orchestra, made up of his pupils, a mandolin, a flute, a cornet, etc. Then the grocer's son would give a recitation and the milkman's little wife would repeat the latest music hall novelty. Max Weber would sing Handel. Violin solos by the master would interlard the program with the Polka des Bébés, Cécilette *and the* Rêve d'un Ange *(mazurka).*

These gatherings ("informal and artistic" Rousseau called them) were attended by the intelligentsia as well as artists. Georges Duhamel, Jules Romains, Francis Carco and always Guillaume Apollinaire could be found with Picasso, Braque, Max Jacob and the critics, André Warnod and Maurice Raynal. Foreigners (all foreigners were "Americans" to Rousseau) like the Russians, Baroness Oettingen (who painted under the name of Angiboult and as "Roch Grey" later wrote a poetic volume on the artist), her brother Serge Jastrebzoff (Ferat), the German critic and art dealer, Uhde, the Italian painter, Ardengo Soffici, were constant guests. When Max Weber was about to leave for America, a special soirée was given on December 19, 1908. During this period Rousseau's "Saturdays" became almost as celebrated as Mallarmé's "Tuesdays" in the rue de Rome had once been.

So great was the interest in Rousseau on the part of the younger artists that in 1908 a fantastic "banquet" was tendered in his honor in Picasso's studio in the rue Ravignan. Picasso had picked up an early portrait (*Mlle M.*) by Rousseau for a few francs in a junk shop and this became the excuse for a more or less spontaneous party where, in addition to many of Rousseau's friends already mentioned, the company included Leo and Gertrude Stein. The evening was a gay one, even though dinner failed to appear, Picasso having given the wrong date to the caterer. There were extravagant toasts and speeches, Rousseau played on his violin, the guests sang, and Apollinaire improvised a poem beginning, "You remember, Rousseau, the Aztec landscape. . . ." The painter was overcome with emotion, and the tears ran down his face as he listened to the praise of his admirers.

Though Rousseau now concentrated on exotic landscapes, finding a ready response for them which in turn encouraged him to paint more and more ambitiously, he varied his excursions into these fantasies with occasional pieces of genre. Only Rousseau, with his folk sincerity and self-taught principles of composition, could have carried through to success *A Game of Football* (page 51) shown at the Independents in 1908. There is something festive and ballet-like in these four figures seen against a luminous autumn landscape reminiscent of other richly surfaced views of the same time. Against the squared-off field, with rows of trees placed at either side like columns, the players, in striped jerseys, are depicted in jaunty movement, their poses rhythmically linked, one to another, the staccato of the hands repeated in four distant trees. Judged by the standards of Salon realism, *A Game of Football* was a preposterous affair, and there were many to judge it such, among them certain admirers who had learned to accept the stylizations of his tropical landscapes. To those who saw deeper the picture could be related to the traditions of Tournai tapestries and the frescoes at Avignon.

The Cart of Père Juniet (page 53), painted the same year, is one of Rousseau's most clarified and subtle translations of that middle-class milieu which made up his daily life. By comparing

A Game of Football (Joueurs de Football). *1908 (dated). Oil, 40 x 32 inches. Lent by Paul Rosenberg and Co.*

it with a photograph[1] of the models (page 53) one can see how the painter managed at the same time to enlarge the spatial significance, order the color, and still preserve to an extraordinary degree the poetic homeliness of the original subject. Max Weber, who watched him paint it, relates that at one time when he saw the picture on the easel, all of the canvas was covered with the exception of a white space left for the dog underneath the cart. "Aren't you making that dog too large?" he inquired. Rousseau looked musingly at the picture. "No, it must be that way," was the painter's answer. It is this intuitive certainty of the rightness or wrongness of a pictorial element which more and more marks the final development of Rousseau's art.

His happiness was rudely shattered early in 1909 when he became mixed up with an unscrupulous former pupil who used the aged painter in a scheme to cheat the Bank of France.[2] The swindle was discovered; and though obviously innocent, Rousseau found himself haled into court and facing a serious charge. Terrified, the painter is said to have offered his counsel the whole contents of his studio, with its many unsold canvases, if he would only get him off. At the trial the lawyer produced the artist's scrapbook with its long series of damaging *critiques* and, to the surprise and hilarity of the court, displayed one of his pictures, *Monkeys in the Forest*, to show what a hopeless innocent the defendant was. But the Bank of France is a serious institution and Rousseau was found guilty and sentenced to two years' imprisonment. Fortunately the sentence was remanded. Bowing to the judge, the relieved artist remarked, "I thank you deeply, Monsieur le Président, I will paint the portrait of your wife."

An increased freedom to move within the picture space and still retain a simple, dominant design is found again in the small canvas, *Mother and Child* (page 54). Two flowering branches, in place of elaborated trees, bend over the heads of the figures, and notes of salmon, vermilion and blue are instinctively balanced by the gleaming black of the mother's dress. The little still lifes (page 55) with their sensitive color and impeccable clarity show his respect for the object, no matter how humble. In the smaller of the two the mouse gnawing at the candle is a characteristic touch. On its reverse is an inscription: "Gift to my friend Weber, the 20th of August, 1908, union of America and France, the 2 republics."

The *Portrait of Joseph Brummer* of 1909 (page 59), one of the last he did, shows his friend and dealer seated in a wicker chair before a background of trees, closely allied to the extravagant foliage of the jungles. It is a mistake to think of such a setting as merely a decorative convention to fill space. For Rousseau the landscape element was quite as important as the figure. When engaged on the portrait of Apollinaire, the artist selected a background from the Luxembourg Gardens. "I've found a pretty corner, very poetic." (Letter of August 31, 1908.) The poet appeared for his first sitting and the artist carefully measured "my nose, my mouth, my ears, my forehead, my hands, reducing them to the dimensions of the stretcher." This method of working, which suggests a tailor rather than a painter, has been often quoted to prove

[1] A comparison made by J. J. Sweeney in his *Plastic Redirections in Twentieth Century Painting*, Chicago, The University of Chicago Press, 1934, p. 15 and reproduced here by his kind permission.

[2] Wilenski (bibl. 63) gives the only full account of this episode, page 245, and Appendix IV, 376–7.

52

The Cart of Père Juniet. 1908 (dated). Oil, 38¼ x 50¾ inches. Collection Madame Paul Guillaume, Paris. Not in the exhibition.

Photograph of the Juniet family and the cart. Courtesy of James Johnson Sweeney.

Mother and Child. 1905–08 (?). Oil, 8¾ x 6½ inches. Collection Max Weber.

Rousseau's incredible naïveté. But such an obeisance to reality liberated him for his significant problem: how to objectify the figure before him and still harmonize it with those strict pictorial laws which his intuition demanded. Except in the little sketches before nature, his method was never instantaneous. It was a slow, additive exploration. Organizing his impressions into broad planes, he continually strove for greater clarity. To Uhde he remarked of a picture in process, "Don't you believe I ought to make the leaves in the first plane a little clearer?" His feeling for the permanent made him seek out a severe linear pattern to which he

54

The Pink Candle. 1905–08 (?). Oil, 6¼ x 8½ inches. Collection The Phillips Memorial Gallery.

Still Life. 1900–08 (?). Oil on wood, 2⅞ x 5½ inches. Collection Max Weber.

Fisherman. 1909–10. Oil, 14½ x 17½ inches. Collection Dr. and Mrs. Harry Bakwin.

constantly opposed passages of invented color and relieving areas of gray and black. The picture was not finished until every form had its proper stability and tension.

In a way he was as lost as Cézanne without nature. During the course of the portrait his letters to Apollinaire implore him to come to the studio to pose. The background is done but the figure needs more attention; the paint will dry in and then it will be double the work. "I have had many difficulties . . . You didn't come back to pose and I was bothered about certain tones but I finished it, nevertheless, from memory." (Letter of August 3, 1909, page 76.) He demanded the model before him to check and control his vision. Lacking it, he could not realize the individuality of forms, the special sense of their character. "Never forget nature, Weber," he used to remark again and again to the young painter.

By the time he portrayed Joseph Brummer he knew just how to proceed. Compare the reworked face of the *Portrait of a Young Girl* (page 26) with the broadly designed features in this later example. The feeling for grandeur which permeates his final style condenses the

56

Spring in the Valley of the Bièvre. 1908–10 (?). Oil, 21½ x 18 inches. Collection The Metropolitan Museum of Art.

multiplicity of nature into a solid, monumental expression. Psychologically the model is invested with the calm but intense gentleness that we find in all of Rousseau's portraits.

About this time the first serious, if somewhat ironic, consideration of Rousseau to appear in print was published in *Comœdia* for April 3, 1909 (bibl. 2). The writer was an official critic, Arsène Alexandre, but he went so far as to admit that "if they weren't so expensive I would like to have some of these pictures, not to hang them up on the wall, for they exercise a dangerous fascination, but to look at from time to time when we need to be reminded of sincerity. If he had possessed the thing he was utterly lacking in: knowledge, and if he had been able, at the same time to preserve his freshness of conception, Rousseau would be the Paolo Uccello of our century."

The final year of Rousseau's life was an extremely full one. Uhde and Vollard had begun to buy his pictures. Three of his works, including the *Merry Jesters* (page 48), were shown in St. Petersburg and Rome. Though concentrating on jungle themes, he continued his portraits and city views up to the very end, still setting down his first impressions for landscape in preliminary sketches.

Comparison of sketch and finished picture (pages 60 and 61) gives us valuable insight into his way of working. The little study before nature is a rapidly brushed reaction to the scene. The main masses of dark and light are already established but not in any positive arrangement. This quick and ragged brushwork makes no concession to the demands of picture-making. There it differs strikingly from the apparently negligent, but often exquisite, touch of the Impressionists. However, this capturing of atmosphere, this blurring and running together of form, ally it to the methods of Impressionism. The slaty blues and grays and fastidious touches of black might almost have been dashed down by Manet.

Rousseau now starts to build. The sketchy contours are stiffened, made more regular. All that he feels about one of his favorite spots in Paris makes him wish to create a permanent statement. New verticals are introduced, relating the motif to the frame, and the whole composition is given a fulcrum by moving the little figure directly to the center. Only a few lines are used but these lock the linear pattern securely. (Note, for example, how a tree in the middle has been given a triangular shape to repeat in reverse the ship's rigging, and how the arc of the bridge is reiterated.) Gone is the blurred form and atmosphere. The strong illumination of the sky sharpens each silhouette and clarifies each shape. Where the color had been tonal with a tendency toward blues and greens, warm tans and browns now appear to complete the harmony. The red note of the flag (the addition of which plays so vital a part in the design) does much to balance the greens, adding as well its note of animation.

Subtly Rousseau flattens out the uncertain space of the sketch into a system of parallel planes and sensitive intervals. The windows, the high lights on the trees and the rings on the parapet are related in a new rhythm. Seeing the sketch and completed picture side by side reveals again how the artist chose his method and his own stylizations.

Such stylizations reach their climax in the paintings of tropical fantasy, most of them done during the last five or six years of his life. These were the works that brought recognition in his

Portrait of Joseph Brummer. 1909 (dated). Oil, 45¾ x 35 inches. Collection Dr. Franz Meyer, Zürich. On extended loan to The Museum of Modern Art, New York.

Notre Dame from the Quai Henri-Quatre. 1909. Oil, 8½ x 11 inches. Lent by Julius H. Weitzner.

time and established his later fame. The subjects are curiously savage. For *The Hungry Lion* . . . Rousseau wrote a poetic explanation printed in the catalog of the Autumn Salon of 1905: "The hungry lion, throwing himself upon the antelope, devours him; the panther stands by, anxiously waiting the moment when he can claim his share. Birds of prey have ripped out pieces of flesh from the poor animal who pours forth his death-cry! Setting sun." In other pictures a tiger rushes at natives or an ape attacks an Indian (page 67). It would seem that a lingering strain of Delacroix' fierce animal combats—a strain repeated in Salon painting of African and Oriental subjects down the century—makes its reappearance in Rousseau. But if the theme is the law of the jungle, the artist's development is detached and remote. The incident of the struggle is overwhelmed by a luxuriant flora which completely dominates the picture. In some of these works Rousseau treats monkeys at play (pages 48 and 72) but the effect is strange and sub-humorous. His conception answers the reality of imagination rather than of nature.

60

Notre Dame. 1909 (dated). Oil, 13 x 16 inches. Collection The Phillips Memorial Gallery.

In stressing Rousseau's method of composition it would be unwise to overlook his early impressions of Mexico. While he seldom mentioned his years in America, he did remark that the French soldiers were forbidden to eat the tempting fruits. Does the profusion of oranges and bananas in many pictures recall some such injunction? Rousseau referred to his jungles as "Mexican pictures" and Max Weber relates that when the Mexican Ambassador was in Paris, the painter vainly tried to reach him in an effort to sell one of his works. Furthermore one can imagine that behind the curious enlargement of leaves and flowers lie half-forgotten memories of the extraordinary landscape round Vera Cruz.

But if the impulse came to him across the years, it came not as total recall but as a feeling to be verified by nature. Scientists have identified a number of the plants in these canvases, all of them probably available at the Paris conservatory, suggesting that Rousseau studied his exotic flora firsthand. Weber came upon him one day when he was painting. Around his palette

Vase of Flowers. 1901–02. Oil, 13 x 18½ inches. Collection William S. Paley.

Flowers in a Vase. 1909 (dated). Oil, 18⅜ x 13¼ inches. Collection The Buffalo Fine Arts Academy, Albright Art Gallery.

was entwined a small branch of leaves and the artist was studying their form and color minutely. The animals, too, are readily identifiable and we know that as in the case of the owl (page 39) he made direct studies in the Zoo.[1]

His approach was far from literal. Inspired by his vision he arbitrarily rewove the appearance of nature to suit his purpose. The long series of imaginative paintings show Rousseau obsessed by one repeated scheme of composition. He imagines a strongly lighted distance against which he silhouettes darker forms of tree or foliage. Plane upon plane is piled up in intricate design, and usually two small figures focus the eye on the foreground. This same "dream picture" haunted him from the days of *Carnival Evening* (frontispiece) to the last jungle picture he painted.

These final canvases show the self-taught artist wholly in command of his style. The minute elaboration of a passage which he loved and which in certain early pictures breaks up the larger rhythms and forms is here replaced by an all-over spatial design. If we study the right-hand section of *The Jungle: Tiger Attacking a Buffalo* (page 49), we find it amazingly complex. One cutout plane is laid over another and yet another, but Rousseau's control is now so sure that all is directed and unified. Soffici, who watched him paint, tells us that he filled in all the greens, then all the reds, then all the blues etc. (bibl. 47). He had conceived the picture in such precise relationship that he could estimate how many days it would take him to finish a canvas.

At last he was able to interlock figures and landscape and unite their diverse movements. The tiger in *The Jungle* (page 49) has stripes which not only repeat the surface design of the leaves, but his diagonal movement is linked with the three-dimensional broken stalks in the foreground just as the solid weight of the buffalo is bound up with the heavy bunches of bananas that hang downward. All of this takes place in a setting of tremendous magnification. A branch becomes a towering tree and flowers are as prodigiously large as lions. This distortion of natural scale lends a peculiar emotional overtone to the whole composition.

Rousseau's technique has now become free and without apparent labor. Occasionally a retouching shows where he has altered a branch or inserted a leaf but the sureness of execution matches the sureness of conception. While still preserving the effect of precise detail, these canvases are mostly finished in a broad painter-like stroke. In *The Waterfall* (page 65) an even illumination floods the picture; in other examples Rousseau's conventionalized striping of forms with bands of light gives an almost stereoscopic clarity. The color is daringly balanced

[1] Professor Charles E. Olmstead of the Department of Botany of the University of Chicago, who kindly studied photographs of several pictures, has made the following report: "The plants are conventionalized and most of them are difficult to identify. In *The Dream* (page 68) the large peltate leaves and the enormous flowers could be one of the waterlily group. The strap-shaped leaves in the lower right-hand corner belong to the genus *Sansevieria*, native to Africa, but now used extensively as a house plant in temperate regions, and probably escaped in the American tropics. In *The Jungle: Tiger Attacking a Buffalo* (page 49) the large bunches of fruit on the left and center and the very large leaves must be bananas, and the leaf just below the bunch in the center might be *Ceratozamia*, a genus of Cycads. The highly conventionalized tepee-shaped plants in *The Waterfall* (page 65) and *Exotic Landscape* (page 67) might be either *Yucca* (New World) or *Dracena* (mostly Old World). The leaves in the upper right-hand corner of the latter picture are probably those of one of the numerous palms."

The Waterfall. 1910 (dated). Oil. 45½ x 59 inches. Collection The Art Institute of Chicago. Helen Birch Bartlett Memorial.

Exotic Landscape: Ape and Indian. 1910 (dated). *Oil, 45 x 64 inches. Lent by Wildenstein & Co., Inc.*

The Dream. 1910 (dated). Oil, 80 x 118½ inches. Collection Sidney Janis.

68

(see the red leaves in *The Waterfall*) or repeated with an almost musical effect (the oranges in *Exotic Landscape*, page 72).

Such works possess a vitality which goes beyond decoration. Each has its special mood. The battle of ape and Indian in *Exotic Landscape* (page 67) takes place in a setting of sharply cut leaves, repeating the significance as well as the pattern of the spear and spiked headdress, while a blood-red sun and red blossoms echo the tragedy. This use of form and color, symbolically, explains part of the fascination of his last great work, *The Dream* (page 68), painted in 1910 and exhibited in that year at the Independents.

In spite of increasing fame Rousseau's last years were saddened by one disappointment. At sixty-three he fell madly in love with a dour widow ten years younger who seems to have encouraged him for a while, then thrown him over. In vain Rousseau wrote her passionate letters and squandered what money he could get on jewelry. Her family, of the same social status as his own, was horrified by his attentions. They could not forget the scandal of his trial and they considered his claims to being a painter absurd. Rousseau went round to Apollinaire and Vollard, securing witnessed letters to prove that he was an accepted artist. But Madame Léonie, who was employed in a department store where Rousseau often vainly went to see her, would have nothing more to do with him. At his death he left an unexecuted document, willing her most of his pictures, but she did not even attend his funeral.

His awakened amorous spirit found sublimation, perhaps, in *The Dream*, to which he attached a poem:

> *Yadwigha in a lovely dream,*
> *Having most sweetly gone to sleep,*
> *Heard the snake-charmer blow his flute,*
> *Breathing his meditation deep.*
> *While on the streams and verdant trees*
> *Gleam the reflections of the moon,*
> *And savage serpents lend their ears*
> *To the gay measures of the tune.*

(Translated by Bertha Ten Eyck James)

There is a tradition that in his youth Rousseau had been enamored of a Polish woman named Yadwigha. At any rate a character of that name appears in his five-act drama, *The Revenge of a Russian Orphan* (page 76).

His last great effort is a creative résumé of his entire career. In *The Dream* he mingled the moonlight of *Carnival Evening* (frontispiece) and *The Sleeping Gypsy* (page 33) with the nude of *An Unpleasant Surprise*, and set the figure of Yadwigha on a red sofa in the midst of a jungle. This mixture of incongruous elements surprised even his friends and caused a sensation in the Independents. To a critic, André Dupont, who wrote for an explanation, Rousseau replied: "The sleeping woman on the sofa dreams that she is transported into the forest, hearing the music of the snake-charmer. This explains why the sofa is in the picture." But though the

Detail of The Dream. Collection Sidney Janis.

70

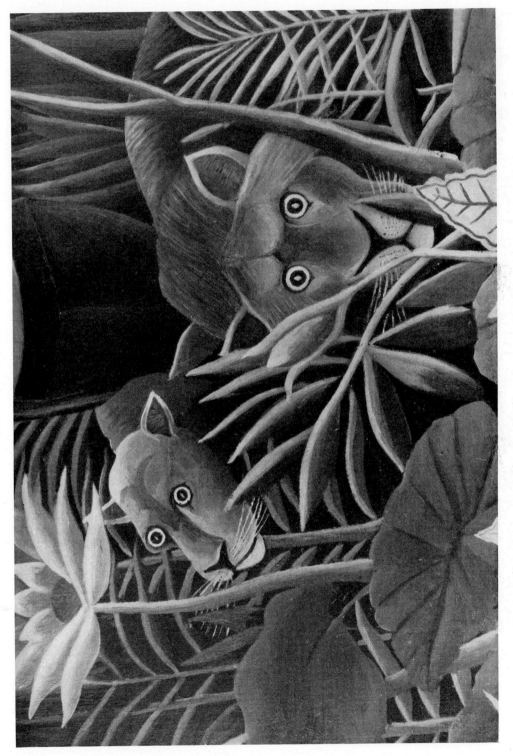

Detail of The Dream. *Collection Sidney Janis.*

Exotic Landscape. 1910 (dated). Oil, 51 x 64 inches. Collection Colonel Robert R. McCormick.

motif was thus cleared up for the literal, Rousseau was so much the artist that to André Salmon he confided: "The sofa is there only because of its glowing, red color."

The Dream is a summation of all those qualities which make Rousseau inimitable. Its organization of spaces and complex tones (an artist counted over fifty variations of green alone) is equaled by its sentiment. The plane of reality (the figure on the sofa) is inventively joined to the plane of the dream (the jungle). In it appears, in heightened form, every symbol of the last ten years of Rousseau's life, redesigned and related with a free intensity. The nude figure surrounded by enormous lilies is one of Rousseau's most perfect realizations (detail, page 70), while the leopards peering from the jungle leaves are full of his expressive mystery (detail, page 71).

"Tell me, M. Rousseau," Vollard asked him, "how did you get so much air to circulate among those trees and the moonlight to look so real?"

"By observing nature, M. Vollard," replied the painter, true to his ideal to the last.

As he prepared the picture for exhibition, Rousseau expressed himself as pleased. To Apollinaire he wrote: "I have just sent off my big picture; everyone likes it. I hope that you are going to employ your literary talents to avenge me for all the insults and injuries I have received." (Letter of March 11, 1910.) These words, spoken at the end of his life, are one of the few indications we have of how much Rousseau had suffered from being misunderstood.

On September 4, 1910, he died at a hospital in Paris at the age of sixty-six. His friends were out of the city and only seven people attended his funeral, among them Paul Signac, President of the Independents. A year later a tombstone was set up by Robert Delaunay, Apollinaire and M. Quéval, his landlord. And in 1913 Brancusi and the painter Ortiz de Zarate engraved on the stone the epitaph that Apollinaire had written:

> *Hear us, kindly Rousseau.*
> *We greet you,*
> *Delaunay, his wife, Monsieur Quéval and I.*
> *Let our baggage through the Customs to the sky,*
> *We bring you canvas, brush and paint of ours,*
> *During eternal leisure, radiant*
> *As you once drew my portrait you shall paint*
> *The face of stars.*
>
> (Translated by Bertha Ten Eyck James)

DANIEL CATTON RICH

1844 Born May 20 at Laval, Department of Mayenne, France.

1862 Probably went to Mexico as a regimental musician in the French army sent by Napoleon III to aid Maximilian.

1866 Returned to France.

1867 Demobilized. Became a lawyer's clerk, entered the customs (?).

1870 Served in the French army in the Franco-Prussian War.

1871 Employed in a toll station on outskirts of Paris as a minor inspector, a post he retained until 1885.

1880 First dated paintings.

1885 Retired on small pension to become a professional painter. Lived in Plaisance Quarter, Paris. A widower, he remarried.

1886 Began to exhibit at the Salon of the Independents, showing continuously until his death in 1910, with the exception of the years 1899 and 1900. *Carnival Evening.*

1890 Painted *Myself. Portrait-Landscape.* Acquaintance with Gauguin, Redon, Gustave Coquiot, Seurat and Pissarro.

1891 *Storm in the Jungle,* his first use of exotic material.

1892 *The Centenary of Independence* (see sketch, *The Carmagnole*).

1895 Commissioned by Rémy de Gourmont to draw lithograph for *L'Imagier.*

1897 *The Sleeping Gypsy.* (Offered in 1898 to his birthplace, Laval, for two or three hundred francs but refused by the town.)

1901 *An Unpleasant Surprise.* Was living at 2 *bis* rue Perrel, Paris.

1904 *Scouts Attacked by a Tiger,* return to tropical theme of *Storm in the Jungle.*

1905 *A Wedding in the Country.* Began to exhibit at the Autumn Salon with three pictures, among them the large and important *Hungry Lion . . .*

1906 Met Robert Delaunay, Vlaminck, Picasso, Guillaume Apollinaire et al. Exhibited at the Independents *Liberty Inviting the Artists to Take Part in the 22nd Exhibition by Independent Artists.*

1907 Commissioned by Madame Delaunay to paint *Snake-Charmer,* which when exhibited at the Autumn Salon elicited praise. Acquaintance with Max Weber and Wilhelm Uhde, later to become his biographer. Joseph Brummer sells a few of his works.

1908 Began Saturday *soirées,* attended by artists and intelligentsia of Paris. Picasso and his friends give Rousseau a banquet in Picasso's studio in the rue Ravignan. *The Cart of Père Juniet.*

1909 January 9. Tried for complicity in fraud connected with the Bank of France. Convicted but due to age and obvious innocence in worldly affairs, sentence was remanded.

1910 Unsuccessful love affair with Madame Léonie. Painted *The Dream.* Died, September 4.

1911 Retrospective exhibition, Salon of the Independents. Biography by Uhde appears.

One-man Exhibitions of Rousseau's Work

1910 NEW YORK, 291 Fifth Avenue (Alfred Stieglitz Gallery)—November 18 to December 8. Paintings and drawings belonging to Max Weber.

1911 PARIS, Quai d'Orsay (Pont de l'Alma), 29th Salon de la Société des Artistes Indépendants—April 20 to June 13 (extended to June 30). One gallery devoted to Rousseau.

1912 PARIS, Galerie Bernheim jeune—December 25 to January 11, 1913. 50 paintings and drawings.

1923 PARIS, Galerie Paul Rosenberg—June.

1925 PARIS, Grande Maison de Blanc—October.

1926 BERLIN, Galerie Flechtheim—March. 32 paintings.

1926 LONDON, Lefèvre Gallery.

1931 NEW YORK, Marie Harriman Gallery—January 2 to February 12. 31 paintings.

1933 BASEL, Kunsthalle—March 1 to April 2. 56 paintings, 8 drawings.

Writings by Rousseau

Un voyage à l'Exposition de 1889. Vaudeville in 3 acts, 10 scenes. Date unknown, probably soon after 1889.

Excerpts printed in Le Bulletin de la Vie Artistique, 3 no8: 181–4 Ap 15 1922; no9: 206–9 My 1 1922. From the manuscript in the possession of Robert Delaunay. Two scenes are of special interest, one in the Louvre, another in the Jardin des Plantes.

[Short autobiography.] 1895.

First published by Soupault (no 50 below), reprinted by Wilenski (no 63 below). Rousseau's own account of his career up to 1895.

La vengeance d'une orpheline russe (in collaboration with Mme. Barkowsky), drama in 5 acts, 19 scenes. Date unknown.

Printed in full in Orbes no2 spring 1929; no3: 101–6 spring 1932; no4: 49–57 winter 1932–3. Excerpts in Flechtheim (no 24 below) and in Wilenski (no 63 below). Mentions Yadwigha as one of the characters, contains another character named Henri, and has considerable material on the glories and horrors of war. Nothing is known of the collaborator.

L'Etudiant en goguette (in collaboration with Victor Louis Rivière), comedy in 2 acts, 3 scenes. Date unknown.

An unpublished manuscript in the possession of Richard Aberle Florsheim, Chicago. The title page is apparently in Rousseau's handwriting, the text in another hand. Nothing is known of the collaborator.

[Letters by Henri Rousseau.] Les Soirées de Paris. 3 no20: 30–64 Ja 15 1913.

Important letters to Guillaume Apollinaire and others. Other letters in Soupault (no 50 below).

[Poems by Henri Rousseau.] Les Soirées de Paris. 3 no20: 65 Ja 15 1913.

Three poems written as legends to his paintings.

Bibliography

The arrangement of this bibliography is alphabetical, under the author's name whereever possible. Catalogs of exhibitions in public museums are listed under the name of the city where the museum is located, while private exhibition galleries are listed under the name of the gallery. The bibliographical form is modelled upon that used in the Art Index.

ABBREVIATIONS: Ap *April*, Ag *August*, D *December*, ed *editor*, F *February*, Ja *January*, Je *June*, Jl *July*, Mr *March*, My *May*, N *November*, no *number*, O *October*, p *page(s)*, S *September*.

SAMPLE ENTRY for magazine article. RAYNAL, MAURICE. Le "banquet" Rousseau. Les Soirées de Paris 3 no 20:69–72 Ja 15 1913.

EXPLANATION. An article entitled "Le 'banquet' Rousseau," by Maurice Raynal, will be found in Les Soirées de Paris, volume (année, Jahrgang) 3, number 20, pages 69 through 72 inclusive, January 15, 1913.

1. AJALBERT, JEAN. La leçon du Douanier. Beaux Arts p 1, 5 O 1 1937.

    Reprints early criticism on Rousseau.

2. ALEXANDRE, ARSÈNE. [Notice on Rousseau] Comœdia (Paris) Ap 3 1909.

    Cited incompletely by Huyghe (no 31). Condescending but not unfriendly notice published during Rousseau's lifetime.

3. APOLLINAIRE, GUILLAUME. Le Douanier. Les Soirées de Paris (Paris) 3 no20:7–29 Ja 15 1913.

    Important source material by the well-known poet and early defender of Rousseau.

4. ——— Il y a. p17–19, 97–100, 146, 152–78, 192–3 Paris, Messein, 1925.

5. BASEL. BASLER KUNSTVEREIN. Henri Rousseau. 16p 1933.

6. BASLER, ADOLPHE. Pariser chronik. Der Cicerone 15:839–40 1923.

7. ——— Recollections of Henri Rousseau. The Arts 11:313–19 Je 1927.

8. ——— Henri Rousseau (sa vie—son oeuvre). 52p Paris, Librairie de France [1927].

    List of paintings, p4–6; bibliography, p12. Also issued with imprint New York, Weyhe [1927]. Sympathetic account of his art and life along with some personal recollections.

8a. ——— Henri Rousseau. 8p Paris, Librairie de France, n.d. (Les albums d'art Druet.)

9. ——— Henri Rousseau. 63p Paris, Editions de la Nouvelle Revue Française, 1929. (Les peintres français nouveaux no34.)

9a. BELL, CLIVE. Since Cézanne. p49–56 New York, Harcourt, Brace, 1922.

10. BRAQUE, GEORGES, AND OTHERS. Testimony against Gertrude Stein. 15p The Hague, Servire Press, 1935.

    Supplement to Transition no23 Jl 1935. Contains "corrections" on Gertrude Stein's version of the Rousseau banquet.

10a. CANN, LOUISE GEBHARD. An artist of the "people." International Studio 81: 251–6 Jl 1925.

11. CHASSÉ, CHARLES. Les fausses gloires; d'Ubu-Roi au Douanier Rousseau. La Grande Revue (Paris) 111:177–212 Ap 1923.

    This and the following (no 12) are malicious accounts of Rousseau's art and reputation, attempting to explain his vogue as a hoax. They contain much valuable contemporary reference.

12. ——— Les défenseurs des fausses gloires; les amis du Douanier Rousseau. La Grande Revue (Paris) 114:439–63 My 1924.

13. CLARETIE, JULES. [Account of the Rousseau trial.] Figaro Ja 10 1909.

14. COQUIOT, GUSTAVE. Les indépendants 1884–1920. p130–33, 208 Paris, Ollendorff [1920].

   History of the Independents with special reference to Rousseau's representation.

15. DELAUNAY, ROBERT. Henri Rousseau le Douanier. L'Amour de l'Art 1:228–30 1920.

16. Dodici opere di Rousseau. 4p Firenze, Libreria della Voce, 1914. (Maestri moderni.)

17. DZITTYA, EMIL. Henri Rousseau. Hamburg, Asmus Verlag, 1924.

   Reference from Huyghe's bibliography (no 31).

18. EDDY, ARTHUR JEROME. Cubists and post-impressionism. p37 Chicago, McClurg, 1914.

19. EGGER, CARL. Der stil Henri Rousseaus; zur erinnerung an die ausstellung in der Basler Kunsthalle im März 1933. Basler Kunstverein Jahresbericht 1932. p3–16 [1933].

   Highly important study of Rousseau's style based on works in the Basel exhibition.

20. —— Henri Rousseau-ausstellung in der Basler Kunsthalle. Die Kunst 67:225–9 My 1933.

21. EICHMANN, INGEBORG. Five sketches by Henri Rousseau. Burlington Magazine 72:300, 302–3, 307 Je 1938.

   An important study of Rousseau's method.

23. FELS, FLORENT. Notes on the Rousseau exhibition at the Marie Harriman Gallery. Formes no11:10–12 Ja 1931.

24. FLECHTHEIM, ALFRED, GALERIE, BERLIN. Ausstellung Henri Rousseau. 39p 1926.

25. GAUTHIER, MAXIMILIEN. La maison natale du Douanier Rousseau; l'association des amis d'Henri Rousseau, d'accord avec la municipalité de Laval, va faire apposer une plaque commémorative sur la maison du peintre récemment découverte. Beaux Arts p 1, 3 D 3 1937.

26. —— Henri Rousseau et Alfred Jarry seront célébrés à Laval, leur ville natale en juin prochain. Beaux Arts p 1, 5 F 11 1938.

27. GEORGE, WALDEMAR. Le miracle de Rousseau. Les Arts à Paris no18:3–11 Jl 1931.

28. GREY, ROCH. Souvenir de Rousseau. Les Soirées de Paris 3 no20:66–8 Ja 15 1913.

29. —— Henri Rousseau. 29p Rome, Editions de "Valori Plastici," 1922.

   In French. Edition with English text, 1924. Sympathetic, if too poetical, account by a personal friend and painter.

29a. GROHMANN, WILL. Henri Rousseau. In U. Thieme & F. Becker, eds. Allgemeines lexikon der bildenden künstler 29:113 Leipzig, Seemann, 1935.

30. HARRIMAN, MARIE, GALLERY, NEW YORK. Exhibition Henri Rousseau. 12p [1931].

30a. Henri Rousseau, le Douanier. 6p London, The Studio, 1936. (The world's masters.)

31. HUYGHE, RENÉ. La peinture d'instinct; introduction. In R. Huyghe, ed. Histoire de l'art contemporain; la peinture. p 185–8 Paris, Alcan, 1935.

   Bibliography, p195–6.

32. KOLLE, HELMUD. Henri Rousseau. 15p Leipzig, Klinkhardt & Biermann, 1922. (Junge kunst, band 27.)

   Text first published in Jahrbuch der jungen Kunst p201–12 1921.

33. LHOTE, ANDRÉ. Exposition Henri Rousseau. Nouvelle Revue Française 21:627–9 N 1 1923.

34. —— L'art populaire. Nouvelle Revue Française 16:274–6 Ag 1 1929.

35. MICHAILOW, NIKOLA. Zur begriffsbestimmung der laienmalerei. Zeitschrift für Kunstgeschichte 4no5–6:283–300 1935.

36. NEW YORK. THE MUSEUM OF MODERN ART. Masters of popular painting; mod-

ern primitives of Europe and America. p39–44 1938.

Text by Maximilien Gauthier, Jean Cassou, and others. Bibliography, p50–1.

37. OLIVIER, FERNANDE. Picasso et ses amis. 231p Paris, Stock, 1933.

Personal reminiscences of Rousseau.

38. PARIS. MUSÉE DE GRENOBLE. Les maîtres populaires de la réalité. 72p 1937.

39. RAYNAL, MAURICE. Le "banquet" Rousseau. Les Soirées de Paris 3 no20:69–72 Ja 15 1913.

40. ———— Picasso. p52–60 München, Delphin Verlag, 1921.

41. ———— Picasso. p44–52 Paris, Crès, 1922.

42. ROH, FRANZ. Ein neuer Henri Rousseau; zur kunstgeschichtlichen stellung des meisters. Der Cicerone 16:710–16 Jl 1924.

Also published in Jahrbuch der jungen Kunst p57–60 1924.

43. ———— Zum begriff der laienkunst; malereien eines matrosen. Der Cicerone 17:470–1, 473–5 My 1925.

44. ———— Henri Rousseaus bildform und bedeutung für die gegenwart. Die Kunst 55:105–14 Ja 1927.

Also published in Die Kunst für Alle 42:104–14 1927.

45. SALMON, ANDRÉ. Propos d'atelier. p137–48 Paris, Crès, 1922.

Reminiscences and recollections by an early defender.

46. ———— Henri Rousseau dit le Douanier. 140p Paris, Crès, 1927. (Peintres et sculpteurs.)

47. SOFFICI, ARDENGO. Henry [sic] Rousseau. La Voce (Florence) 2 no40:395–6 S 15 1910.

The first serious study of Rousseau. Written just before his death.

48. ———— La France jugée à l'étranger; le peintre Henry [sic] Rousseau. Mercure de France 87:748–55 O 1910.

A translation of no 47, with a prefatory note by Lucile Dubois.

49. SOUPAULT, PHILIPPE. La légende du Douanier Rousseau. L'Amour de l'Art 7:333–7 O 1926.

50. ———— Henri Rousseau, le Douanier. 59p Paris, Editions des Quatre Chemins [1927].

Contains Rousseau's autobiographical note and letters.

51. STEIN, GERTRUDE. The autobiography of Alice B. Toklas. p126–32 New York, Harcourt, Brace, 1933.

52. TROHEL, JULES. Origines mayennaises du Douanier Rousseau. Mercure de France 205:710–14 Ag 1 1928.

53. UHDE, WILHELM. Henri Rousseau. 66p Paris, Figuière, 1911.

First French edition of the first biography by Rousseau's friend and dealer. Full of important biographical material and first-hand impressions.

54. ———— Henri Rousseau; herausgegeben durch die Galerie Alfred Fletchtheim, Düsseldorf. 67p Düsseldorf, Ohle, 1914.

First German edition. A part of the books issued later in Germany, in 1921 and 1923 (nos 56–57).

55. ———— Henri Rousseau. Deutsche Kunst und Dekoration 47:16–26 O-N 1920.

56. ———— Henri Rousseau. 89p Dresden, Kaemmerer, 1921. (Künstler der gegenwart, band 2.)

Revised German edition of Uhde's 1911 book (no 53) with fewer and different plates and some additional text.

57. ———— Henri Rousseau. 2. auflage. 89p Berlin & Dresden, Kaemmerer, 1923. (Künstler der gegenwart.)

Second edition of revised publication.

58. ———— Picasso and the French tradition. p41–6 Paris, Editions des Quatre Chemins; New York, Weyhe, 1929.

Original in French: Picasso et la tradition française. Paris, Editions des Quatre Chemins, 1928.

59. Uhde, Wilhelm. Henri Rousseau et les primitifs modernes. *In* R. Huyghe, ed. Histoire de l'art contemporain; la peinture p189–96 Paris, Alcan, 1935.

Excellent account of Rousseau's art and its place in the development of modern painting.

60. ——— Von Bismarck bis Picasso; erinnerungen und bekenntnisse. p150–2, 156–8, 247–54 Zürich, Oprecht, 1938.

Personal recollections by Rousseau's first biographer.

61. Vollard, Ambroise. Recollections of a picture dealer. p93–4, 196, 215–19 London, Constable, 1936.

Translated by Violet M. MacDonald. Also issued with imprint Boston, Little, Brown, 1936. Anecdotes by the famous dealer.

62. Warnod, André. Les berceaux de la jeune peinture. p50, 84, 185, 230 Paris, Michel, 1925.

63. Wilenski, R.H. Modern French painters. p80–2, 119–20, 134–5, 181–3, 205–7, 243–7, 360–3, 372–7, and passim New York, Reynal & Hitchcock, 1940.

The most complete account of Rousseau's career and art. Contains material on the trial and excerpts from his drama, *La vengeance d'une orpheline russe.* Bibliography, p360–1.

64. Zervos, Christian. Henri Rousseau et le sentiment poétique. Cahiers d'Art 1 no9:227–36 1926.

65. ——— Rousseau. 96p Paris, Editions "Cahiers d'Art," 1927. (Les grands peintres d'aujourd'hui no2.)

66. ——— Histoire de l'art contemporain. p99–112 Paris, Editions "Cahiers d'Art," 1938.

67. Zürich. Kunsthaus. Les maîtres populaires de la réalité. p11–12, 17–19 1937.

Exhibition catalog. Text by W. Wartmann.

ELEVEN THOUSAND FIVE HUNDRED COPIES OF THIS BOOK HAVE BEEN PRINTED IN JANUARY 1942 FOR THE TRUSTEES OF THE MUSEUM OF MODERN ART BY THE PLANTIN PRESS, NEW YORK

lavender

lavender

growing and using in the home and garden: practical inspirations for
natural gifts, recipes and decorative displays

Tessa Evelegh

photographs by Debbie Patterson

LORENZ BOOKS

FOR ANN
THE ULTIMATE LAVENDER BAG

This edition is published by Lorenz Books

Lorenz Books is an imprint of Anness Publishing Ltd
Hermes House, 88–89 Blackfriars Road, London SE1 8HA
tel. 020 7401 2077; fax 020 7633 9499
www.lorenzbooks.com
info@anness.com

© Anness Publishing Ltd 1996, 1999. 2001 updated 2002

Published in the USA by Lorenz Books, Anness Publishing Inc., 27 West 20th Street, New York, NY 10011; fax 212 807 6813

Published in Australia by Lorenz Books, Anness Publishing Pty Ltd
Level 1, Rugby House, 12 Mount Street, North Sydney, NSW 2060. tel. (02) 8920 8622; fax (02) 8920 8633

This edition distributed in the UK by Aurum Press Ltd
25 Bedford Avenue, London WC1B 3AT. tel. 020 7637 3225; fax 020 7580 2469

This edition distributed in the USA by National Book Network
4720 Boston Way, Lanham, MD 20706. tel. 301 459 3366; fax 301 459 1705; www.nbnbooks.com

This edition distributed in Canada by General Publishing
895 Don Mills Road, 400–402 Park Centre, Toronto, Ontario M3C 1W3. tel. 416 445 3333; fax 416 445 5991; www.genpub.com

This edition distributed in New Zealand by David Bateman Ltd
30 Tarndale Grove, Off Bush Road, Albany, Auckland. tel. (09) 415 7664; fax (09) 415 8892

Publisher: Joanna Lorenz
Project Editor: Joanne Ripon
Designer: Nigel Partridge
Photographer: Debbie Patterson
Styling: Tessa Evelegh
Illustrations: Anna Koska
Production Controller: Joanna King

*Additional Pictures supplied by: The Bridgeman Art Library: p18; Bruce Coleman Ltd: p8 (Herbert Kranawetter), p20 (C. Martin Pampaloni); The Garden
Picture Library: p16, p19, p28 (left & right), p32. p33. p35 (left & right); Clive Nichols: p34; Visual Arts Library: p10.*

Printed and bound in Singapore

5 7 9 10 8 6 4

CONTENTS

INTRODUCTION

Prized down the centuries for its perfume, medicinal properties and rich violet hues, lavender has been the darling of all herbs since time began. Amongst its many qualities, it is thought to calm irritable children and relieve insomnia, anxiety and depression – in other words, to create a wonderful sense of well-being. Certainly, the past few months, working with lavender for this book have been most pleasurable, and never before has work been such a joy. Whether it was because the lavender was working its magic on me, or whether it is because its colour, perfume and form make it such a versatile and pleasurable material to use, I will never know. But I hope I have been able to pass that pleasure on to others in the ideas and projects throughout the book.

For me, lavender has particular poignancy. It takes me back to my school-days in Devon where lavender grows in rich, abundant hedges in front of almost every garden. Bewitched by its perfume as I walked through the Devon country lanes, I was never able to resist picking just a few spikes to take home. I used to lay the flower heads on a tray to dry, then make a lavender bag for my mother – one each year. Those lavender bags are long lost – a casualty of many house moves – but there was no shortage of new ideas for this book, together with endless other uses for lavender.

One aim of this book was to make everything very doable, bearing in mind that often our lifestyles leave little space for time-consuming handicrafts. The other aim was not only to acknowledge lavender's rich and respected past, but also to give it a future with a fresh new look. Lavender's association with Victorian England is wonderfully romantic, but its sculpturally spiky form, intoxicating perfume and varied shades have now brought its potential far beyond the confines of simply scenting Grandma's linen chest.

ABOVE: Collecting lavender from the quilt-like fields of England's last remaining commercial lavender farm in Norfolk.

RIGHT: As the sun sets over a field of lavender the wonderful perfume scents the warm, summer evening air.

CHAPTER ONE

HISTORY AND FOLKLORE

STOECHAS IS AN HERB WITH SLENDER TWIGGES
HAVEING YE HAIRE LIKE TYME, BUT YET LONGER LEAVED
AND SHARP IN YE TASTE AND SOMEWHAT BITTERISH.

DIOSCORIDES, ABOUT AD 60

ABOVE: White lavender is a beautiful foil to the purple varieties.
*LEFT: Native to the countries of the Mediterranean, lavender has
grown alongside olive trees for centuries.*

ABOVE: Lavender helped to save the city of Jerusalem from destruction when used by Judith to stupefy the enemy army commander, Holofernes.

Lavender's glorious hues and beguiling aromatic perfume have ensured it a place in the hearts of men and women almost since time began. In the course of this long-lived love affair, all sorts of properties, both real and imaginary, have been attributed to it.

As well as for its unmistakable perfume, lavender has been recognized since Roman times for its healing and antiseptic qualities, its ability to deter insects, and for washing. There are many references in the Bible to the high price of lavender, using its ancient name of spikenard. In the gospel of St Luke, the writer reports: "Then took Mary a pound of ointment of spikenard, very costly, and anointed the feet of Jesus, and wiped his feet with her hair: and the house was filled with the odour of the ointment."

Over the centuries, biblical references and folklore became entwined. It was believed that Adam and Eve took lavender with them when they were banished from the Garden of Eden. According to legend, it was not until much later that lavender received its distinctive perfume, bestowed upon it by Mary when she laid the baby Jesus' clothes on a bush to dry.

It was perhaps because of the Virgin's saintly touch that lavender came to be regarded as a safeguard against evil. Traditionally, a cross made from lavender was hung over the door for protection. In some respects, to our ancestors' minds, lavender really did ward off evil in that it appeared to guard against disease. During the Great Plague in London in the seventeenth century, it was suggested that a bunch of lavender tied to each wrist would protect against infection. It is known that the grave-robbers, who plundered plague victims' personal belongings, used to wash in Four Thieves Vinegar, which contained lavender. Although the thieves must have come into contact with the infection more than most people, they rarely contracted the disease. In sixteenth-century France, too, lavender was considered an effective and reliable protection against infection. For example, glove-makers, who were licensed to perfume their wares with lavender, escaped cholera at that time.

Nowadays, rather than its antitoxic qualities, lavender is associated with love. Certainly, in folklore, the aroma of lavender seemed to promote an almost drunken stupor in some hapless males. In one of the apocryphal books of the Bible, Judith anointed herself with perfumes including lavender before seducing Holofernes, the enemy commander. Once he was under her heavenly-scented influence, she murdered him and saved the city of Jerusalem.

By Tudor times, lavender seemed to have established a hot line to Cupid. If a maiden wanted to know the identity of her true love, she would sip a brew of lavender on St Luke's day, while murmuring:

St Luke, St Luke, be kind to me,
In my dreams, let me my true love see.

Alpine girls tucked lavender under their lovers' pillows, hoping to turn their thoughts to romance, and once married, newly-weds would put bunches of dried lavender under their mattresses to ensure marital passion.

BENEFICIAL LAVENDER

STOECHAS ... OPENETH THE STOPPINGS OF THE LIVER, THE LUNGS, THE MILT, THE MOTHER, THE BLADDER
AND IN ONE WORD ALL INWARD PARTS, CLENSING AND DRIVING FORTH ALL EVILL AND CURRUPT HUMOURS.

THE HERBALL, JOHN GERARD, 1597

For centuries, the herbs of the countryside were the people's medicine chest, and the healing qualities of lavender have always given it a leading role. The first record of its remedial properties dates back to AD 77 when the Greek Dioscorides, a military doctor, wrote, "Ye decoction of it ... is good for ye griefs in ye thorax." About the same time, a Roman, Pliny the Elder, declared that lavender helped the pains of those who were bereft, those with menstrual problems, upset stomachs, kidney disorders, jaundice and dropsy. He also noted that it eased insect bites. The Roman soldiers were so impressed with its healing qualities that they took it with them on their campaigns to dress their war wounds.

Later, in the Middle Ages, it was the monks and nuns who nurtured herbs, using them to make medicines. An abbess from Mainz, Hildegarde, noted in the twelfth century, what the Romans knew centuries before, that oil of lavender was effective in treating head lice; a method that was still being used in 1874 on children in Provence. During the sixteenth century Queen Elizabeth I of England was a devotee. She drank copious cups of lavender tea to treat her frequent migraine headaches.

During the seventeenth century, lavender secured its place in the herbals as pretty much a cure-all, relieving headaches, calming nerves, healing acne, and soothing insect stings and "the bitings of serpents, mad-dogs and other venomous creatures".

By the nineteenth century, lavender appeared in the London Pharmacopeia as an ingredient of palsy drops, which supposedly remedied "falling sickness, cold distempers of the head, womb, stomach and nerves against apoplexy, palsy, convulsions, migrim, vertigo, loss of memory, dimness of sight, melancholy, swooning fits, acne and barreness in women".

More recently, during the First World War, modern antiseptics were in such short supply that the public were asked to gather garden lavender so the oil could be used together with sphagnum moss to dress war wounds.

LEFT: Herbalists and pharmacists have been using lavender remedies since ancient times.

ABOVE: Lavender has been grown domestically for home remedies and decoration for centuries.

Lavender is still used in herbal remedies. Cushions filled with dried lavender can help to induce sleep and ease stress or depression. It can be brewed into a tea, which is then either drunk, used to make compresses for dressing wounds or for applying to the forehead to relieve congestion of the sinuses, headaches, hangovers, tiredness, tension and exhaustion.

Although herbal remedies are natural, they can be dangerous if used incorrectly, so it is best to take lavender internally only in the form of a weak tea, unless you are being treated by a registered herbalist.

TO MAKE A COMPRESS

Soak a clean cloth in a hot infusion of lavender and use immediately.

TO MAKE AN INFUSION OR TEA

Pour boiling water into a cup, let it cool for 30 seconds, then add a teaspoonful of fresh or dried lavender. Cover and leave to steep for ten minutes, stirring occasionally. Strain and drink lukewarm.

The antiseptic qualities of a weak infusion of lavender tea help to cleanse the system and to relieve headaches and stomach upsets. Sweeten it with a little honey if you prefer.

AROMATHERAPY

LAVENDER ... IS NOT ONLY SWEET OF SMELL, AND THEREFORE COMFORTABLE TO THE BRAINE,
BUT ALSO GOOD FOR THE PALSIE AND ALL OTHER INFIRMITIES.

HAVEN OF HEALTH, THOMAS COGHAM, 1584

Although the word "aromatherapy" is a new one, first appearing in the 1920s in an article by chemist René-Maurice Gattefosse, the practice of it goes back many thousands of years. The Greek physician, Theophrastus, who lived during the third century BC, wrote about the healing qualities of scent in his book, *Concerning Odours*. The effect of aromas was obviously recognized from early times. Lavender was used for strewing, to sweeten the air, fumigate sick areas and in incense for religious ceremonies. Contemporary aromatherapists believe that odours can affect the chemical balances in the body, which could account for the mood-changing properties of aromatic herbs such as lavender.

Lavender oil earned itself a special status in modern aromatherapy, ever since Gattefosse treated a gangrenous laboratory burn on his hand with pure lavender oil and it healed remarkably quickly. He had previously noticed that severe war wounds could become infected and the poison enter the bloodstream, yet when treated with lavender oil, the poisons were detoxified and the wounds themselves healed remarkably quickly, making for a rapid overall recovery.

Aromatherapy depends on using essential oils, extracted by distillation. This is not easy to accomplish successfully at home, so most people prefer to buy them. Pure lavender oil is expensive, but it is not worth being tempted by any offered at lower prices. This is often an indication that the oil has been blended with other oils which are not as effective in aromatherapy. It is best, therefore, to buy bottles that are marked "Pure Lavender Oil" from reputable suppliers.

HOW TO USE ESSENTIAL LAVENDER OIL

There are many beneficial ways to use lavender oil, but as with all essential oils, it is highly concentrated and should be treated with respect. Never take it internally, and never use it to treat children under 18 months.

In a burner

Scent the air with a romantically aromatic fragrance by burning lavender oil. Wonderful both inside or out at any time of the year, it is particularly beneficial in the summer as it also repels insects. It relaxes the mind and relieves headaches too.

You can buy specially made porcelain burners. The top consists of a shallow bowl and under this there is a compartment to take a small candle. Put 15ml/1 tbsp warm water on to the bowl, and add a few drops of the essential oil. Light the candle, then sit back and enjoy the perfume. You will need to top up the water regularly so the bowl does not burn dry. Burners should never be left burning unattended, should never be left in a child's room and should never be left alight after you go to sleep.

In the bath

A lavender bath is deeply relaxing, mildly antiseptic and helps to heal tiny cuts and scratches,

BELOW: Lavender, mixed with oil for massage, releases an aroma which will help ease stress headaches and promote calm and restful sleep. It also helps muscular aches and pains. Warm the oil slightly before you begin, to release the scent.

bites or swellings. It is also a thoroughly enjoyable way to end any day, whether you have had a hot summer ramble along country lanes or a stressful day at work.

Add five to ten drops of lavender oil to a warm bath, then lie back and luxuriate!

For massage

Lavender oil blended with a base massage oil such as almond oil, sunflower oil or olive oil can be great for relaxing and de-stressing. Blend it in the proportion of two to three drops of essential lavender oil to 5ml/1 tsp of base oil. For larger quantities, use 20–60 drops of lavender to 105ml/7 tbsp base oil.

As an inhalation

To clear a stuffy nose, or to help to clear skin blemishes and acne, make a facial steam bath.

Add five to eight drops of essential lavender oil to a bowl of hot, steaming water. Lean over the bowl with a clean towel covering your head and the bowl and gently inhale.

FIRST AID WITH LAVENDER OIL

You can also use neat lavender oil drops as an antiseptic, to help to heal cuts and grazes, for inflammation including those from burns, boils, acne, dermatitis and eczema; to soothe

ABOVE: Lavender repels insects, and when warmed in a burner also creates an evocative ambience.

sunstroke, insect and animal bites; and to lift the spirits. Here are some of the ways in which lavender can be used for first aid.

Acne

Blend two drops of pure lavender oil into your normal unscented moisturizer to help to heal stubborn spots and pimples.

Burns

A drop of lavender oil on superficial burns or scalds will help to relieve the pain and make for a quick recovery.

Colds

Add a few drops of lavender oil to a warm relaxing bath to help to eliminate the toxins. When you get out, you could dab a drop of

lavender oil under each nostril. The camphorous odour can help to clear mucus.

Congestion

Relieve a congested nose by putting a few drops of essential lavender oil on your handkerchief to inhale when needed during the day. At night, you could put the handkerchief on your pillow by your nose, or use a lavender sleep pillow (see below), which will also decongest your nose as you sleep.

Headaches

Dab a drop of lavender oil on each temple to help relieve migraine and other headaches.

Insect bites

Take the sting out of bites with a drop of essential lavender oil.

Sleeplessness

Make up a lavender pillow to lay on your pillow next to your nose as you drift off to sleep. The aroma will relax you, inducing drowsiness.

Sunburn

Add a few drops of lavender oil to still mineral water, and use an atomizer to spritz it on to sore skin.

THE ANCIENTS

MY SWEETHEART, MY BRIDE IS A SECRET GARDEN, A WALLED GARDEN,
A PRIVATE SPRING ... THERE IS NO LACK OF HENNA AND NARD.

SONG OF SOLOMON, ABOUT 900 BC

Precious, aromatic lavender has been highly valued since ancient times. The Egyptians learned how to make intoxicating perfumes that almost certainly included lavender. When Tutankhamun's tomb was opened in 1922, some 3,000 years after it had been sealed, urns were found, filled with unguent that still retained traces of lavender fragrance. In those days, this valued unguent would probably have been used only by royal families or the high priests who dispensed them.

Women have always known about the power of perfume in seduction. The Queen of Sheba, trying to close a deal with King Solomon, offered gifts of frankincense, myrrh and spikenard. And Cleopatra seduced both Julius Caesar and Mark Antony with the help of perfumes including lavender.

Scenting the body was certainly not the sole prerogative of women in those days. Wealthy men in Ancient Egyptian times used to put solid cones of unguent on their heads, and as these slowly melted, they would cover their bodies with the precious heady perfumes. The Greek philosopher Diogenes in the third century BC preferred to start at the bottom, anointing his feet, rather than his head, with perfume. "When you anoint your head with perfume, it flies away in the air, and birds only get benefit of it," he reasoned, "whilst if I rub it on my lower limbs it envelopes my whole body, and gratefully ascends to my nose."

The Romans were outrageously lavish with fragrances, using aromatic oils liberally to perfume their hair, bodies, clothes and beds, and of course in their famous public baths housed in magnificent buildings. Bathing became something of a ceremony, starting with first an oiling in the *unctuarium,* followed by a cold

bath in the *frigidarium,* a tepid one in the *tepidarium* and a hot one in the *caldarium.* While in the hot bath the Romans would pour warm fragrant oils over themselves, prior to a body massage with aromatic oils. Roman women bathed at home before anointing themselves with nardium, a fragrant, lavender-based compound. At night, they hung lavender next to their beds probably as much to deter the bedbugs as to entice any prospective suitors.

Lavender's many names date from ancient times: in his seventeenth-century *Herbal Simples,* Dr Fernie noted, "By the Greeks, the name Nardus is given to Lavender, from Naards, a city of Syria near the Euphrates". Spike refers to the shape of the flowers, and sometimes lavender was known as Indian spikenard. The Romans would recognize stoechas lavender, which they named after the Islands of Stoechades, now the Iles d'Hyères, just off the coast of the French Riviera.

LEFT: A sundial becomes a striking focal point when fringed by white lavender, then enveloped by a double line of mauve, which itself creates a boundary between two parts of the garden.

RIGHT: In ancient times lavender's pointed blooms inspired its early name of "spikenard".

OLDE ENGLAND

LADIES FAIR, I BRING TO YOU, LAVENDER WITH SPIKES OF BLUE;
SWEETER PLANT WAS NEVER FOUND, GROWING ON OUR ENGLISH GROUND.
CARYL BATTERSBY, EARLY TWENTIETH CENTURY

In medieval Britain, it was the monks who preserved the knowledge of herbal lore in their diligently tended physic gardens. Way back in 1301, lavender is listed among the herbs grown at Merton Abbey. This was perhaps the first hint of the role the surrounding region would play in the history of English lavender. Situated in the centre of Mitcham, this whole area was, by the middle of the nineteenth century, blanketed in rolling fields of purple lavender, making it the very epicentre of English lavender oil production. This was the cradle of all the associations of lavender, England and the Victorians.

The move from physic gardens to domestic gardens really came about after King Henry VIII of England dissolved the monasteries in the sixteenth century. Lavender began to regain the same popularity it had had in Roman times, with the ladies of manor houses making their own preparations of sweet waters in their still-rooms for gifts in times of celebration. Once again, lavender was associated with cleanliness and was strewn among linens, sewn into sweet bags, used to freshen the air and mixed with beeswax to make furniture polish.

Queen Elizabeth I adored lavender, not just to ease her migraine, but as a perfume, for which she paid dearly – £40 to a distillery for

ABOVE: An engraving depicting a street vendor selling lavender, a fairly common sight in those days, taken from Modern London *by Richard Phillips, published in 1804.*

a single compound. This encouraged the development of lavender farms and a continued growth of lavender products. Henrietta Maria, the wife of King Charles I, brought Continental

cosmetics to the English court, introducing the idea of perfuming soap with lavender oil, making pot-pourri and using lavender waters for washing and bathing.

Once again, lavender joined forces with Cupid. The famous nursery rhyme "Lavender blue, dilly dilly", is derived from a more bawdy version, written in 1680, where everyone is set to work:

Some to make hay, diddle diddle
Some to the corn
Whilst you and I, diddle diddle
Keep the bed warm.

It was during the seventeenth century that the great herbalists, Gerard, Parkinson and Culpeper wrote their herbals, generating considerable public interest in all herbs. Lavender sellers became part of the street scene, asking high prices for their wares, especially during the Great Plague of 1665 when it was thought to protect against the terrible disease.

But it is Victoria's long reign that is most associated with lavender. The queen was so enthusiastic about this versatile aromatic herb that she appointed Miss Sarah Sprules "Purveyor of Lavender Essence to the Queen", and would make personal visits to Miss

RIGHT: This simple parterre of clipped box and lavender makes a focal point in a lawn.

Sprules' lavender fields in Wallington. The queen's homes were impregnated with the aroma of lavender. It was used to wash floors and furniture, and lavender bags were slipped between the sheets in linen presses. Victoria's love of lavender made it a fashionable fragrance among English ladies throughout the land. Those who could not afford the essence would buy fresh lavender annually from the sellers in the streets, encouraged by the now famous cries, including this:

> *Come buy my lavender, sweet maids,*
> *You cannot think it dear,*
> *There must be profit in all trades,*
> *Mine comes but once a year.*
>
> *Just put one bundle to your nose,*
> *What rose can this excel;*
> *Throw it among your finest clothes,*
> *And grateful they will smell.*

In London, the lavender was sold mainly by gypsies who brought it up from the fields of Mitcham. As well as selling it fresh, they would use dried lavender to make up gifts such as muslin bags for wardrobes, and smaller ones for young women to wear in their cleavage, in hope of attracting a suitor.

Lavender was also used to repel insects, treat lice, to perfume pot-pourri, furniture polish and soap, and as a cure-all in the household medicine cupboard. Victorian ladies, it seemed, never grew tired of the fragrance of lavender and, sadly, this contributed to its waning popularity in the early twentieth century during which it became associated with old ladies. But as interest gradually returned to things natural in the latter half of the century, lavender has seen a another revival.

A WORLD OF LAVENDER

IT IS THE WONDER AND JOY OF THE SOUTH IN ITS BLUE DRESS
AND ITS SCENT IS GOD'S GIFT TO EARTH.
MAURICE MESSEGUE, 1972

Native to Persia and the Canaries, with some species originally hailing from all around the Mediterranean, India, Nigeria, Sudan, Yemen, Saudi Arabia, Iran, Oman and Ethiopia, lavender thrives in heat and dust. It is endowed with narrow, hairy leaves and a

BELOW: A wonderful spiky bush of lavender, growing in a Tuscan garden in Italy.

plentiful supply of oils to protect it from drying out. It is surprising, therefore, that in Victorian times, it was Mitcham, now a London suburb of back-to-back terraces, that was the English centre of lavender oil production. Its sunny south-facing, well-drained slopes were clothed in amethyst, exuding the heady fragrance that had become known as quintessentially English.

Lavender not only thrived in England's relatively damp and chilly climate, it excelled. The combination of long summer days and harsher conditions encourage the plant to make more oil. English lavender produced the finest oil and fetched up to 200 shillings a pound in 1881, while French and Dutch oils cost a mere 18 shillings. English lavender products became known the world over, largely due to old-established companies, such as Yardley's and Potter and Moore, which sold lavender waters and lavender soaps.

The lack of the endless hot sunny days of lavender's native climate has obviously never been a problem for English varieties. Way back in the seventeenth century, John Parkinson noted among his herbals that French lavender was "somewhat sweete, but nothing compared with lavender", and Mrs Leyel, founder of the Society of Herbalists, wrote in 1931 that she had "often come across fields of French Lavender in bloom, and that the scent has been poor compared with English Lavender grown under the worst conditions".

Even so, a combination of disease and the pressure of ever-increasing land values meant that suburban terraces gradually replaced the lavender fields of Mitcham, Wallington and Carshalton. The English lavender industry

would have been long extinct, had it not been saved by Linn Chilvers, a nurseryman in Norfolk. In 1932, he decided to try growing lavender on a commercial scale. When he died, his trustee, Adrian Head and his wife, Ann, took an active role in the business. Ann is still a director and their son, Henry, is Managing Director, continuing the tradition by nurturing 40.5 ha/100 acres of rolling fields of lavender for the distillation of pure English lavender oil.

It is the sun-baked slopes of Provence, around Grasse, the centre of the perfume industry, that now reigns as the world largest lavender producer. Originally brought to the area by the Romans, lavender took a liking to the southern slopes of the Alps with their well-drained soil, and began to grow wild in the region. By the turn of the twentieth century,

LEFT AND ABOVE: The Norfolk lavender farmhouse in all its summer glory, surrounded by blooms.

local shepherds collected it for sale to the perfumers of Grasse, but it was still not cultivated. However, the perfume houses and the French government saw that lavender could provide a means of stopping people leaving

the area for the cities. With this double backing, just before the First World War, they cleared the almond orchards and planted lavender in its place. Provence had staked its claim as the world's leading lavender producer.

There are now many other producers of lavender around the world, including Spain, the Netherlands, Belgium, Germany, Bulgaria, Russia, Australia, Japan, Canada and the United States.

In North America, it was the Shakers who first grew lavender commercially. This strict breakaway sect of the English Quakers set out to be self-sufficient when they arrived in New England, and developed well-maintained herb farms. These herbs and the resulting medicines made in the Shakers' own pharmacies were sold to the "outside world" in beautiful simple packaging that very often listed all the ingredients of the contents, which was unusual at the time.

Lavender was a favourite herb for gift items as well as medicines. Backed by slick New York advertising in the last century, and respected for the honest quality of their goods, Shaker produce soon found its way back to England. Even today, a few lavender items made by the remaining Shaker communities and specialist Shaker craftspeople are sold around the world.

CHAPTER TWO

CULTIVATION

FRENCH LEVENDER BEING A HERBE OF VERY GOOD SMELL,
AND VERY USUAL IN LANGUEDOC AND PROVENCE,
DOTH CRAVE TO BE DILIGENTLY TILLED IN A FAT GROUND
AND LYING OPEN TO THE SUNNE.

THE COUNTRIE FARM, RICHARD SURFLEET, 1600

ABOVE: A field of lavender, just ready for harvesting.
*LEFT: Whilst lavender is mostly cut by machine, some is harvested
by hand and transported to the distillery in wooden boxes.*

ABOVE: Lavender fields in bloom emit a fragrance that is as beguiling as the colour is rich.

Few people could not be seduced by the sight and fragrance of a lavender field in full bloom. The bushes, laid out in rows like a magnificent amethyst quilt enveloping the land, provide a memorable experience, made all the more powerful by the intoxicating aroma and the persistent humming of bees.

Lavender was not always cultivated like this. For a long time, especially in the south of France, it was not cultivated at all, rather it was gathered from the hills by shepherds and local people who supplied the perfumers of Grasse. When the French did begin to cultivate commercially, they followed the English pattern of planting the bushes individually with ample space around each one. It was not until the mid-1950s, in anticipation of mechanical cutters, that the bushes were planted in the neat rows we now associate with lavender fields. Nine years later the machines began to ease the toil of harvesting.

However, in Britain, lavender had been cultivated on a much smaller scale for centuries, originally by monks in their well-organized physic gardens for use in various remedies and medicines. Each variety of herb usually had its own separate bed for ease of identification, and this was probably the inspiration for the knot gardens and parterres that first became popular during the time of Elizabeth I.

Despite the fact that lavender is native to the dry climates of the Mediterranean and Middle East, it has never had trouble settling in cooler, northern countries and has become the mainstay of traditional gardens. As well as single bushes, glorious indigo hedges of lavender are common in many parts of Europe.

One of the reasons lavender is so successful in such differing climates is that it hybridizes very readily, and so there is usually a variety that can adapt to suit the local environment. Over the centuries, this has caused much argument among the lavender *cognoscenti,* and even nurserymen have been known to get a variety wrong! To add to the confusion, lavender is sometimes given national names such as English, French, Dutch or Spanish lavender, none of which are actual varieties, merely names given to the variety most commonly grown in the relevant country.

In Britain, there are two main types of lavender that are frost-hardy and happy to be here, and within those two types, there are endless hybrids. The most common garden type is *Lavandula angustifolia,* which used to be sometimes known as *L. vera* or *L. officinalis.* It is a stocky, sweet-smelling plant, carrying just

BELOW: Lines of different varieties of lavender make a rich textural pattern.

one flower spike on each stem. The other main type is *Lavandula x intermedia,* which is a cross between *Lavandula angustifolia* and *Lavandula latifolia,* (a leggy, grass-like plant that grows wild in the Mediterranean). *Lavandula x intermedia* has the frost-hardiness of *L. angustifolia* combined with the camphorous perfume and axial shoots of *L. latifolia.*

ABOVE: While French lavender grows on the slopes of the Alps, English lavender is now cultivated on flatter fields. However, both have the vital well-drained soil needed for lavender cultivation.

Another type that is becoming increasingly popular is *L. stoechas.* The varieties in this group are very easy to recognize since they carry flamboyant, butterfly-like, coloured bracts on top of the flowers. Abundant in the *Iles d'Hyères* off the French Riviera, this type is sometimes known as French lavender and is almost certainly a type the ancient Romans would have recognized. Most of this group is not frost-hardy, and includes several lavenders that have pretty, delicate fern-like leaves.

LAVENDER DIRECTORY

Lavender blue dilly, dilly, Lavender green,
When I am king, dilly dilly, You'll be my queen.
Traditional nursery rhyme

We expect lavender to span a colour range from palest lilac to deepest indigo. But when we start a love affair with it, we find there are green, pink and even white varieties too. Blooms can be tall and spiky or stocky and tightly packed. Leaves can be long and slim or fuller and ferny.

Lavender falls into several types: *Lavandula latifolia,* a grass-like lavender that grows wild in the Mediterranean; *L. angustifolia,* which is stockier and has a fuller flower; and *L.x intermedia,* which is a cross between the two, and is sometimes called lavandin. Another group, *L. stoechas,* has butterfly bracts on top of the flowers, and is sometimes known as French lavender. Some varieties in this type have decorative fern-like leaves. A fourth group is *L. Pterostoechas,* which is not frost-hardy, and sometimes temperamental.

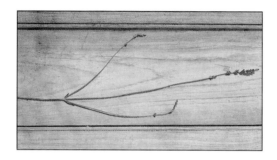

ABOVE: Lavandula latifolia

L. Latifolia types

L. LATIFOLIA is rarely seen in Britain because it is prone to disease, but flourishes in Mediterranean gardens. Its strong camphorous fragrance has formed the basis of the Spanish spike oil industry, being used extensively to perfume furniture wax, air fresheners and polishes.

L. LATIFOLIA X LANATA "SAWYER'S": Large, tapered blooms make this a glorious garden plant.

L. Angustifolia types

L. ANGUSTIFOLIA "IMPERIAL GEM": Similar to 'Hidcote', which is often thought of as English, it is a mainstay of cottage gardens. Popular for its abundant indigo blooms.

L. ANGUSTIFOLIA "NANA ALBA": Also known as dwarf white or baby white. A charming lavender with white blooms on a compact bush that grows only 30cm/12in high.

L. ANGUSTIFOLIA "MISS KATHARINE": A delightful new pink lavender.

L. Intermedia types (Lavandin)

L.X INTERMEDIA "GRAPPENHALL": Traditional English garden lavender with blue purple flowers, both on leading and axial shoots.

L.X INTERMEDIA "GROSSO": A wonderful hybrid with an attractive, large, fat flower named after M Pierre Grosso.

BELOW: Lavandula latifolia x lanata "Sawyer's"

BELOW: Lavandula angustifolia "Imperial Gem"

BELOW: Lavandula angustifolia "Nana Alba"

ABOVE: *Lavandula angustifolia* "Miss Katharine"

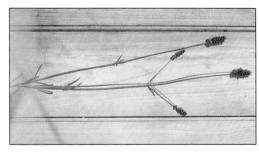

ABOVE: *Lavandula* x *intermedia* "Hidcote Giant"

ABOVE: *Lavandula stoechas viridis*

ABOVE: *Lavandula* x *intermedia* "Grappenhall"

ABOVE: *Lavandula stoechas*

ABOVE: *Lavandula pinnata*

ABOVE: *Lavandula* x *intermedia* "Grosso"

ABOVE: *Lavandula stoechas pedunculata*

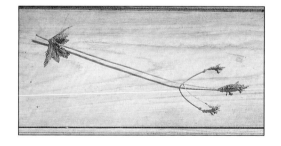

ABOVE: *Lavandula canariensis*

L.x INTERMEDIA "HIDCOTE GIANT": Heavily scented, this large shrub has generous compact flowers, making it excellent for dried arrangements.

L. Stoechas types

L. STOECHAS: A delightful compact lavender which exhibits the distinctive petal-like bracts on top of the flower. This plant is often known as French lavender.

L. STOECHAS PEDUNCULATA: This is a somewhat taller variety of the *stoechas* which also has larger top bracts.

L. STOECHAS VIRIDIS: The small bracts on this beautiful green lavender immediately betray its *stoechas* heritage.

L. Pterostoechas types

L. PINNATA: A delicate-looking, half-hardy plant with small blooms, carrying three blooms on the leading stem and having lower axial shoots. It also has distinctive dentata-style ferny leaves.

L. CANARIENSIS: This is similar to L. *pinnata*, only carrying just one bloom on the leading stem, and having axial shoots.

SOIL AND CLIMATE

BEST AMONG ALL GOOD PLANTS FOR HOT SANDY SOILS ARE THE EVER BLESSED LAVENDER AND ROSEMARY.

GERTRUDE JEKYLL, 1900

Lavender is an extraordinarily versatile and resilient plant. Hailing from the heat and dust of the sun-drenched countries around the Mediterranean, and even the desert regions of Saudi Arabia, the Yemen and Ethiopia, it is truly surprising that it is also happy living in the damp northern climes of the British Isles and even Norway. The reason is that not all varieties are hardy in all climates. While some,

ABOVE: Lavenders in lilac, indigo and white, planted informally and allowed to grow freely, create a natural-looking environment, almost as if they were in the wild.

LEFT: White lavender with indigo 'Hidcote' lavender makes a striking combination.

native to hotter climes, cannot tolerate any frost, others, such as *Lavandula angustifolia*, are hardy and will survive through several degrees of frost.

Whether lavender grows in the heat of the desert or the damp chill of the British Isles, it does need light soil – preferably sand or gravel

in a dry, open sunny position with good drainage so the roots do not get waterlogged in winter. Generally, lavender is not keen on acid soils, preferring chalky ones. If your soil is acid, use lots of garden lime, and add a top dressing annually. If you live in a very heavy clay area, dig a deep hole, line it with shingle

ABOVE: Hot and dry or chilly and damp, lavender can thrive in a surprisingly wide variety of climates without too much attention.

to help the drainage and then add sand to the soil when planting. A little manure added when planting will help to establish the shrubs, but do not add too much as this will stimulate leaf growth rather than creating more flower heads and will also dissipate the fragrance. Not at all difficult to grow, lavender hardly needs any fertilizer as too much nourishment would simply go into growing more leaves which is not the desired outcome.

NURTURING LAVENDER

LAVENDER SPIKE HATH MANY STIFF BRANCHES OF A WOODY SUBSTANCE ... THE FLOURES
GROW AT THE TOP OF THE BRANCHES, SPIKE FASHION, OF A BLEW COLOUR.

THE HERBALL, JOHN GERARD, 1597

It is not difficult to propagate lavender, though, since it naturally hybridizes so readily, it does have some surprising characteristics. Some hybrids are called "mules", and will never produce their own seed, so these have to be propagated by taking cuttings.

TAKING CUTTINGS

In spring or autumn, choose a young shoot about 5cm/2in long, and pull it downward

sharply, so it comes away with a "heel". Dip the heel end of the cutting into hormone rooting compound and plant it in light, sandy compost. Keep it moist and protect it from frost. Spring cuttings root quickest – in about six weeks.

SOWING FROM SEED

Even if you do have a plant that produces seed, you may find its offspring a little unpredictable. Lavender hybridizes so readily that a single bush can produce shrubs of quite different sizes carrying different flowers. Added to this, the seed is not very reliable, so you need to plant plenty of it in April, then prick off the resulting seedlings into their own pots once they are established.

BUYING PLANTS

By far the most reliable and easiest form of cultivation is to buy the young plants, which are available from garden centres or growers. Make sure you know what you are getting by

LEFT: Taking cuttings is an easy, efficient and probably the most reliable way to propagate lavender. The woody cutting on the left is a hardwood cutting, the soft leafy one on the right is a softwood cutting.

ABOVE: Seed can be collected by tying a bag around the heads of ripened lavender to catch it when it falls. It can also be bought from seed companies by post.

buying either well-known varieties or buying when the bush is in bloom.

PLANTING OUT

Young plants can be planted out once the frosts are over. Traditionally, growers allow 60cm/2ft between each plant, though if you are planning a hedge, plant them closer, 30–45cm/12–18in apart. Some experts say that lavender should not be allowed to flower in its first year to encourage a strong, bushy growth. It will produce a full complement of blooms from the second year onwards, and

will reach full size by the fifth year. To help prevent the bush from becoming straggly, at the end of August cut the flower stems right down where they leave the bush. The lavender should be pruned hard in March to encourage a good growth in the summer.

ABOVE: Young plants can be bought at various stages from growers and garden centres.

LEFT: Once the frosts are over, the lavender plants are ready to be planted out.

LAVENDER GARDENS

... AN ARBER FAYRE TO PARADISE, RIGHT WELL COMPARABLE, SET ALL ABOUT
WITH FLOWERS FRAGRANT.

HAWES, 1554

The most glorious gardens stimulate all five senses, and many would say that fragrance comes a very close second to the look of the garden. The very word paradise is said to come from *pairidaeza,* which was the name for enclosed scented gardens in Persia 2,000 years ago. Since some varieties of lavender are native to Persia, it is doubtless that lavender took a starring role in those ancient *pairidaezas.*

Lavender is seeing a resurgence along with cottage-style gardens, many of which have at least one lavender bush in their borders, but there is so much more you can do with this richly fragranced shrub.

If the garden is large enough, you could plant swathes of it, letting it colonize areas of the garden that might otherwise have been a touch scrubby. Its indigo hues in summer and

RIGHT: Swathes of lavender release a heady scent, creating an evocative, memorable ambience for summer days in the garden.

BELOW: Lavender and roses make perfect planting companions, offering delightful combinations of scent and colour. Low-growing lavender can also be used as decorative ground cover for what can be a leggy shrub.

LEFT: *Rows of indigo lavender bushes make spectacular borders for this charming well-stocked herb garden in France.*

RIGHT: *Hedges of lavender release their sweet fragrance as visitors make their way down this English country cottage pathway.*

BELOW: *The distinctive butterfly-like bracts of* Lavandula stoechas *make a delightful sight in a cottage border.* L. stoechas, *sometimes known as French or Spanish lavender, may not be hardy to frost, so it is wise to plant it in a decorative pot like this mosaic one so it can be moved and over-wintered under glass.*

the gentle grey green of the leaves in winter will provide a year-round blanket of colour. In summer too, its pungent aroma will not only attract gently humming bees and butterflies, but repel less welcome guests such as some slugs, flies and millipedes.

Another delightful way of using lavender is to take inspiration from the gardens of yore when it was used in a more formal, architectural way. The English Tudors made intricate knot gardens, creating elaborate patterns of low-clipped box hedges with each section either planted with herbs or filled with coloured gravel. By the seventeenth century, these knot gardens were set together in geometric arrangements that were known as parterres. Nowadays, a mini knot garden or even a parterre, perhaps planted with different varieties of lavender, could make a spectacular feature within the larger framework of the whole garden.

As well as being used within the framework of multi-shrub mini hedging, lavender makes a marvellous indigo hedge itself. Use it as a border for pathways or large flower beds, or let it tumble over a low wall, for example, to create a spectacular boundary to the front garden, striking in both country and city.

HARVESTING AND DISTILLING

... AND AS FOR THE TIME OF GATHERING FLOWERS, LET IT BE WHEN THE SUN SHINES UPON THEM,
SO THEY MAY BE DRY, FOR IF YOU GATHER WHEN THEY BE WET OR DEWY, THEY WILL NOT KEEP.

CULPEPER

A year's work nurturing lavender in the fields all hangs in the balance on the day for harvesting. However carefully the bushes have been planted, pruned and nurtured as

BELOW: Hand sickles were the traditional tool for cutting lavender. They are still used for small sampling jobs and for the lavender that will be sold in bunches. But the main harvest for distilling is now brought in mechanically.

they bloom and produce their precious oil, all can go to waste if the conditions are not right on the day of harvesting. It is not simply a decision based on how ripe the flowers are. When they are ready for harvesting, the weather must be set fair because if it turns damp or rainy even during the harvest, the results will be disappointing.

Gauging the time to commence harvesting is the most critical decision of the year. The flowers have to be fully developed so they contain the maximum amount of oil, but not over-mature when the florets start to drop. A dry spell around the end of July and beginning of August is usually the best time, depending on the weather. Rain is disastrous at harvest time because any damp on the cut lavender will make the florets turn brown and then drop off. Even under the best weather conditions, the lavender has to be gathered quickly and taken straight to the distillation stills as fast as possible before any of the oils have the chance to dry out.

The best time to cut lavender growing in the garden is in the early morning or evening of a fine day, as the midday heat encourages it to release some of its precious scent. Cut the stalks with sharp secateurs, and take the lavender inside immediately, away from the hot sun.

ABOVE: The lavender is tied into bunches as it is cut, and laid on the now-shorn bushes.

Most commercial lavender goes to the distillery. The cut lavender is loaded into the still, steam is passed through, vapourizing the oil, which then cools to become a clear gold liquid. In the hour this takes, 250kg/350lb of lavender produces just 500ml/18fl oz of oil, which must be left to mature for a year.

ABOVE: Lavender destined for the distillery does not need to be tied into neat bunches, so it is loosely bagged up on the machine and taken straight to the stills. There, it is emptied on to the distillery floor and then shovelled into the still.

LEFT: When it is cut and tied in bunches, the lavender is transported to the warehouse and distillery in old wooden crates.

ABOVE: These old copper stills have been distilling lavender oil since 1874, producing a fragrance that experienced perfumers can distinguish from that of oil which is distilled in the more modern stainless steel stills.

BUNCHING AND DRYING

HANGED UP IN HOUSES IN THE HEATE OF SOMMER, DOTH VERY WELL ATTEMPTER THE AIRE, COOLE
AND MAKE FRESH THE PLACE, TO THE DELIGHT AND COMFORT OF SUCH AS ARE THEREIN.

THE HERBALL, JOHN GERARD, 1597

Nothing quite captures the essence of summer so well as dried lavender, which continues to release its fragrance for at least 8 months and, after an initial fading, retains a soft indigo hue. It can be dried in two forms:

BELOW: Lavender destined for drying needs to be bunched up as it is cut.

in bunches for dried flower arrangements, and as florets for filling sachets, cushions, linen bags, wallhangings and even oven gloves.

Commercially, the bunches are tied to a special drying rack that is hoisted up on to the wall of the drying barn. Loose lavender is left in its sacks and warm air is passed through it for two to three days. The florets are then separated from the stalks and sieved several times in a special sifter until only the flowers remain.

At home you should cut blooms for dried arrangements before the florets open; those for pot-pourri, a little later when the oil, and therefore the fragrance, has had time to develop. Make up the lavender into small bunches as you cut it, then secure with elastic bands which will tighten as the lavender shrinks during the drying process. The bunches then need to be hung up in a dry place with plenty of air circulating.

Lavender smells so fabulous and the bunches look so pretty, you can use them to decorate the house. Attached to the bottom of the spindles, hanging into the stairwell all the way up the stairs, for example, they will get plenty of through draught and be safely protected from knocks. If you wish, tie it with decorative twine, ribbon or even scraps of fabric. Drying loose lavender is even easier. Simply

ABOVE: Large bunches of lavender are dried commercially on frames hoisted on to the walls of the drying barn. At home, they can be on strings, or simply hung on any wall where there is plenty of air circulation.

spread it out on trays in a well-aired room. Once the lavender is completely dry, it is easy to strip the florets from the stalks by gently rubbing them between your fingers.

ABOVE: *Rows of lavender bunches hung up to dry always look decorative, even when held together with an elastic band. The bunches should be well spaced to ensure good air circulation which speeds the drying process.*

CHAPTER THREE

LAVENDER AND LINEN

LET'S GO TO THAT HOUSE, FOR THE LINEN LOOKS WHITE
AND SMELLS OF LAVENDER, AND I LONG TO LIE IN A PAIR OF
SHEETS THAT SMELL SO.

THE COMPLEAT ANGLER, IZAAK WALTON, 1653

ABOVE: Lavender is often used to scent pretty bags such as these.
*LEFT: A lavender field in full bloom, just minutes before harvest
begins, is a breathtaking sight.*

The association between lavender and wash day has been a long and often romantic one. Its very name comes from the Latin *lavare*, "to wash", and over the centuries this came to mean clothes and household linens as well as for bath-time use. Lavender's exquisite aromatic smell was its obvious attraction. When dried and strewn in the linen cupboard, it also had the advantage of deterring insects and moths that could spoil the clothes.

Constance Isherwood, in her turn-of-the-twentieth century brochure on the lavender industry, boasted:

Velvet gown and dainty fur,
should be laid in lavender,
For its sweetness drives away
Fretting moths of silver grey.

To have one's clothes stored or "laid up" in lavender meant that they were being given special care … and indeed, by all reports, it was a costly business. In 1592, during Shakespeare's lifetime, Greene noted of one cash-strapped man: "The poore gentleman paies so deere for the lavender it is laid up in, that if it laies long at the broker's house, he seems to buy his apparel twice".

More generally, clothes were strewn with

ABOVE: In warm climates what better way to dry laundry than draped over lavender?

lavender to lend a personal fragrance to the owner. Brides would sprinkle dried lavender in their trousseaux, and William Langham, in the *Garden of Health*, in 1579 suggested that lavender was boiled in water, then, he advised,

"Wet thy shirt in it, dry it again and wear it." And by the time of the London Cries, the lavender sellers exhorted young ladies to:

Come buy my sweet lavender, sweet maids…
throw it among your finest clothes.
And grateful they will smell.

In Italy, and among the Shaker communities in the US in the last century, clothes and linens were laid on lavender bushes in the hot sun to absorb the fragrance.

Before the seventeenth century, lavender was used in the chests of drawers and linen presses of the more wealthy homes to overcome the rancid smell of soap which was not yet perfumed. Nowadays, it is a wonderful way of lending a fresh smell to all household linens and clothes.

Traditionally, young girls and women wove stems of lavender into lavender bottles or sewed sachets to fill with dried lavender flowers. This is still a delightful thing to do, and since these "sweet bags" do not need to be large, they are quick to make. Also, as only scraps are needed, they can be made from extravagantly rich fabrics, such as silks and velvets, satin and lace. Appliqué or embroider them; make them in heart shapes, squares,

ABOVE: Lavender has long been used to scent linen. Place dried bunches in your wardrobe.

triangles or rectangles; make them fancy, or make them "country" simple to suit your individual style. Sachets can be made to lay among the linens and clothes, or with ribbon or wire loops added to hang on coathangers, on the inside of cupboard doors, or even on the outside to scent the whole room.

Lavender sachets and bags are the most satisfying items to make as you really do not need a lot of lavender and the loose dried flowers are perfect, perhaps left over from a dried arrangement or bought in bags. You can, of course, pick the flowers from your garden and dry them yourself, to bring the fresh scent of your own garden into the house to enjoy for the rest of the year. Although it is generally accepted that dried lavender flowers will only continue being fragrant for eight months or so, a gentle squeeze and a shake every so often will release the perfume which keeps the linen sweet for much longer.

S H A K E R   S A C H E T S

━━ ◦═◦ ━━

These delightful country-style sachets are Shaker-inspired, being made in natural cotton checked fabrics and decorated with sprigs of dried lavender. The heart was a favourite Shaker motif, symbolic of their saying: "Hands to work and heart to God". Attached to wires, they can be hung on the inside of a cupboard to scent its contents.

━━ ◦═◦ ━━

MATERIALS
paper and pencil for template
scissors
fabric, at least 50 x 25cm/20 x 10in
pins, needle and sewing thread
loose, dried lavender
wire
6 sprigs dried lavender
raffia or ribbon to tie

1 ⁜ Trace the heart-shaped template or make one about 20cm/8in high. Using this as a pattern, cut out two fabric hearts. With right sides facing, stitch the hearts together around the outside edge, leaving a gap of 5cm/2in on the straight part of one side. Trim the seams to about 5mm/¼in and clip into the seam allowance at intervals around the curves of the heart.

2 ⁜ Turn the heart right side out, fill generously with loose, dried lavender and slip-stitch to close the gap. Bend both ends of a 30cm/12in length of wire into hooks, then fit them into the seam at the top curves of the heart. Bend the wire a little more to close and shape.

3 ⁜ Make two bunches of three sprigs of lavender, using wire to secure, then cross these over each other and wire together. Tie with raffia or ribbon and stitch to the front of the heart.

LACY LAVENDER HEART

The ribbons and lace on this exquisitely pretty, heart-shaped lavender bag lend it a Victorian feel, evoking an era when the rich perfume of English lavender was the most sought after in the world.

MATERIALS
paper and pencil for template
scissors
silky muslin, about 60 x 20cm / 24 x 8in
pins, needle and sewing thread
stranded embroidery thread
pearl button
loose, dried lavender
50cm / 20in antique lace
50cm / 20in very narrow satin ribbon
50cm / 20in ribbon for bow (preferably chiffon)

1 ❧ Make a heart-shaped template about 15cm/6in high. Using this as a pattern, cut out four muslin hearts and tack them in pairs so each one has a double thickness of muslin. Cut a smaller muslin heart and stitch to the front of one of the larger hearts using two strands of embroidery thread.

2 ❧ Make another row of running stitches inside the first row. Using the same thread, sew on the pearl button, then make another row of running stitches inside the other two. With right sides facing, stitch around the edge of the two large double-thickness muslin shapes, leaving a 5cm/2in gap along one of the straight sides.

3 ❧ Trim the seams, then snip into the seam around the curves and snip off the bottom point. Turn the heart right side out, fill with lavender, then slip-stitch to close the gap. Slip-stitch the lace around the edge. Stitch the satin ribbon over the lower edge of the lace. Make a bow with the chiffon ribbon and stitch on to the heart.

LAVENDER BOTTLES

Young ladies in Victorian times used to while away afternoons making lavender bottles by encasing lavender heads in their own stalks, then weaving them with ribbon. Sadly, these charming drawer and cupboard scenters are all but extinct. Although they are not difficult to make, they are fiddly and time-consuming, which means they are not commercially viable. Revive the tradition by making your own, using ribbons in muted colours to complement the lavender. Each bottle uses up a fair amount of ribbon, but since the quantity depends on both the length of the lavender stalks and the width of the ribbon, it is best to buy, say, 2m/2¼yd and make several bottles.

MATERIALS
9 (or any odd number) stalks freshly
picked lavender
1m/1yd narrow satin or rayon ribbon

1 ⬥ Make a bunch of the lavender and, using the ribbon, tie their stalks together tightly at the top.

2 ⬥ Very carefully bend the stalks down one by one over the lavender heads, being careful not to snap them.

3 ⬥ Weave the ribbon in and out of the lavender stalks. When you have covered the heads, wrap the ribbon around the stalks and bind them to their ends. Cover the ends of the stalks with the ribbon, then bind back up the stalks until you reach the heads again. Tie in a knot and a bow to fasten.

BUTTONED
BAGS

The simplest ideas can often be the most effective. These miniature pillows of lavender have been decorated with rows of buttons and toning velvet ribbon to make elegant decorative drawer scenters.

MATERIALS
scissors
scraps of silk, at least 30 x 20cm / 12 x 8in
40cm / 16in velvet ribbon, about 2cm / ¾in wide
6 round buttons, 10mm / ⅓in diameter
2 heart-shaped buttons
needle and sewing thread
loose, dried lavender

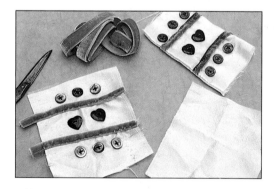

1 ❧ Cut out two pieces of silk about 14 x 10cm / 5½ x 4in and two lengths of ribbon a little longer than the width of the silk. Fold in half lengthways and sew a little more than a third in from each end of one piece of silk. Stitch on the buttons.

2 ❧ With right sides facing, sew the two rectangles together down the long sides. Turn right side out. Use another length of ribbon to bind the bottom of the bag by folding it in half lengthways over the end and tucking in the ends, then sewing through all the thicknesses. Fill the bag with the loose, dried lavender, making sure you don't overfill it. Bind the top in the same way as the bottom.

LAVENDER LINEN BAG

The top of this delightful draw-string linen bag has been filled with lavender to scent its contents sweetly. A fringed edging – in this case cut from a tablecloth – has been used to trim the bottom of the bag.

MATERIALS
1.5 m / 1⅔yd main fabric
1m / 1yd fringing
pins, needle and sewing thread
1m x 10cm / 1yd x 4in organza
1m / 1yd rayon ribbon
2m / 2¼yd 6in grosgrain ribbon
bodkin or large safety pin
chenille knitting yarn
2 large beads
loose, dried lavender

1 ✄ From the main fabric, cut out a 24cm / 9½in circle, two rectangles measuring 50 x 40cm / 20 x 16in and two rectangles for binding measuring 26 x 5cm / 10½ x 2in. Cut the length of fringing in half. Fold the circle in half and mark the fold with pins at either side. Fold it in half the other way and mark with pins. Fold both of the larger pieces of fabric in half lengthways and mark with pins. With right sides facing, match the pin on one piece to one of the pins on the circle. Match the pin on the other piece to the pin on the opposite side of the circle. Sandwich the fringing between the circle and the pieces with raw edges matching. Tack the pieces to the circle, then stitch, leaving the side seams open.

2 ✄ With wrong sides facing, stitch a 10cm / 4in wide strip of organza to the top of the bag. Fold to the outside of the bag. Stitch a length of rayon ribbon over the raw edge. Repeat on the other piece of main fabric. With right sides together, stitch one of the binding strips to the top end of one side of one of the pieces of main fabric, stitching through the layer of organza where applicable. The binding should reach about halfway down the side of the main fabric. Turn over lengthways and stitch to finish binding. Repeat on one side of the other piece of main fabric. Fill the organza channel with lavender from the open end. Bind this in the same way as before. ▶

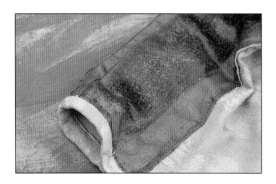

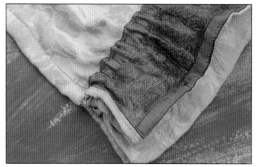

3 ⊱⊰ Fold the whole organza channel to the inside of the bag and stitch through all layers close to the bottom edge of the organza. Make the draw-string casing by sewing another row of stitching to allow for the width of the ribbon.

4 ⊱⊰ With right sides together, stitch the side seams. Use another strip of fabric to bind the seam. Cut the grosgrain ribbon in half and, using a bodkin, thread one piece through the casing. Thread the other piece of ribbon through in the other direction.

5 ⊱⊰ Make a tassel by winding the chenille yarn around four fingers. When satisfied with the thickness, cut the chenille.

6 ⊱⊰ Take another double thickness of chenille and pass through the top of the original chenille. Pass the ends through the hole in the bead and knot tightly at the top. Trim the ends of the tassel and sew it between the two ends of ribbon.

LITTLE LAVENDER CLOTHES HEART

A little heart of lavender is a charming way to scent the wardrobe. It can be fragile, so hang it on the inside or even the outside of the door, where it will not be crushed.

MATERIALS
1m/1yd medium-gauge garden wire
raffia – preferably blue-dyed
1 bunch dried lavender
glue gun and hot wax glue
scissors

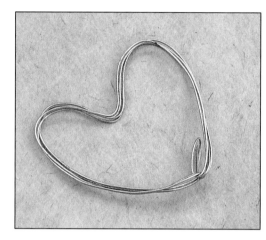

1 ❧ Fold the garden wire in half and half again. Make a hook at one end and hook into the loop at the other end. Make a dip in the top to form a heart shape.

2 ❧ Bind the heart with raffia. Start at the bottom, working round the heart. Tie the ends together.

3 ❧ Starting at the dip at the top of the heart, bind three stalks of lavender to the heart with the stalks pointing inwards and downward. Continue to bind the lavender in bunches of three to the heart, so that they cover the wire, working down the heart. When you reach the bottom, start at the middle of the top again and bind down towards the point. For the bottom, make a larger bunch and glue in position with the flower heads pointing upwards. Trim the stalks close to the heads.

CHAPTER FOUR

DECORATIVE LAVENDER

LADIES FAIR, I BRING TO YOU
LAVENDER WITH SPIKES OF BLUE;
SWEETER PLANT WAS NEVER FOUND
GROWING ON AN ENGLISH GROUND.
CARYL BATTERSBY IN A BUNCH OF SWEET LAVENDER,
CONSTANCE ISHERWOOD, 1900

ABOVE: Sunflowers and lavender make a perfect match.
LEFT: Retaining its rich purple tones, even when dried, lavender
makes a glorious material for arrangements around the home.

LEFT: As well as the much-loved blue shades, lavender comes in palest pink and white.

BELOW: Fresh white lavender is one of summer's rarer delights. Pick it to enjoy when fresh because it does not dry as well as the indigo varieties.

Lavender blues, in hues from deepest indigo through amethyst, violet and hyacinth, all evoke a richness that is well documented throughout history. Purple symbolizes majesty in many cultures. Maybe it is the richness of the colour that makes it so attractive, maybe it is its vast range of shades from pink and red to blue, that means it can be mixed and matched to many other tones. Undoubtedly, purple is an evocative colour, and what better way to use it than with another natural material? As well as the familiar indigo blues, there are the rarer white, pink, and even green varieties which complement the blues.

At its best fresh, lavender needs little fussing. Just bunch it and tie with a simple ribbon, or weave it into a pretty wreath or garland for a special occasion. The effort is worth it as lavender dries readily, even when made up. The Victorians wove garlands of it around the portrait of the head of the family on celebration days. You may not wish to go that far, though a lavender wreath can be fabulous as a wall, table, or church decoration on festive days, and the dried version can serve as a souvenir afterwards.

Dried lavender, too, can make wonderful indoor decorations. Its simple, almost architectural form makes it suitable for a variety of arrangements, that not only look decorative, but scent the room sweetly at the same time. But just as it was in the past, lavender by the bunch is still expensive and because the flowers are tall and spiky-slim, the decorations

use a lot of material. The ideal situation is to have your own lavender hedge so you can cut and dry, building up a stock of material over the summer. You use an extraordinary amount of lavender in making decorations, so if you do not have your own supplies, it would probably be best to adjust the arrangements a little, making smaller displays, rather than using the material too sparsely.

Try to get lavender which has densely packed florets, though the most common variety is usually more feathery in appearance. This works just as well as the densely packed varieties but you have to use much more of it, making it very difficult to estimate the quantities required for the following designs. A bunch or even a specific number of stems can be very misleading. The best solution is to buy as much lavender as you can afford, then work out how much area it would cover by measuring the space taken up by the tips of the flower spikes. Buy a florists' foam base in a size they would easily cover. All the designs on the following pages look just as effective when they are scaled down.

LEFT: Fresh lavender looks stunning on its own in simple containers. Fill several to make a delightful still life.

DETAILS THAT COUNT

⇒⚬⇐

E ven small bunches of lavender can be used decoratively. Tie them – fresh or dried – to the backs of chairs as a scented decoration when entertaining inside or out. As guests brush against the lavender, they will bruise the flowers, so releasing the rich fragrance. Small bunches can be used decoratively in a more permanent way too. Simple bunches can be tied and attached to photograph or picture frames, hung above the bathroom mirror or as a welcome on the front door. Lavender's uncomplicated form calls for uncluttered tying. Think in terms of garden raffia, natural coloured string or twine, or plain narrow ribbons. They all look good.

LEFT: Let the soldier-straight stems of lavender in their exquisite grey-green become part of the decoration. Here two bunches stand guard either side of a driftwood coloured picture frame. Wire the bunches together, tie with coloured string, then secure them in position with a glue gun and hot wax glue.

RIGHT: Bunches of lavender tied with raspberry-coloured grosgrain ribbon to each guest's chair makes a wonderful aromatic, decorative detail when entertaining inside or out. If you first fix the bunches with elastic bands, you can leave them on the chairs as the lavender dries, giving weeks of aroma until all the flowers have fallen.

BAROQUE OBELISK

Evoke the sumptuous style of the seventeenth century with a magnificent be-ribboned obelisk. This is incredibly easy to make and the result is fabulous. However, it does use a lot of lavender and can work out quite costly, so scale it down if you prefer.

MATERIALS
sharp kitchen knife
dry florists' foam cone, about 50cm/20in high
metal urn, about 30cm/12in diameter
dressmakers' pins
2m/2¼yd wire-edged ribbon about
5cm/2in wide
12 dried poppy seed heads
10 large bunches lavender

1 ⋇ Using the kitchen knife, trim the bottom of the florists' foam cone, shaping it to fit snugly into the urn.

2 ⋇ Using the pins, attach the wire-edged ribbon to the foam cone, starting at the bottom and working around to the top, then working back down the cone to make a trellis effect. Scrunch the ribbon slightly as you go for a fuller effect. Position one poppy seed head at the top of the obelisk and others at pleasing intervals on the cone.

3 Cut the lavender stalks to within 2.5cm/1in of the heads and start by inserting in a ring at the bottom of the cone where it meets the rim of the urn. Then, working methodically in rings and lines, gradually fill in each section within the ribbons. As you get near a poppy seed head, remove it so you can insert the lavender near the hole, then replace the seed head.

MOPHEAD TREES

Fashion a pair of enchanting lavender trees, then position them on either side of a mantelpiece mirror or fireplace in a witty allusion to real mophead bay trees growing on either side of a front door.

MATERIALS

FOR EACH TREE
sharp kitchen knife
2 dry florists' foam balls, about
20cm/8in diameter
container, about 20cm/8in diameter
1m/1yd piece contorted willow
5 large bunches lavender
florists' or gardeners' wire
a little reindeer moss

1 ⬩ Using the kitchen knife, cut one of the florists' foam balls in half and place in the container. Use extra foam if necessary to fill the container. Insert two 50cm/20in lengths of contorted willow into the foam.

2 ⬩ Attach the other foam ball to the top of the willow. Choose lavender with similar-sized heads and trim to 2.5cm/1in. Make a ring of lavender round the foam ball, and another in the other direction.

3 ⬩ Fill in each section with lavender, working logically in rows to achieve an even finished result.

4 ⬩ Bend short lengths of wire into hairpin shapes and use to pin the moss into position over the florists' foam in the pot.

HARVEST DISPLAY

The soft bluey-green shades of dried lavender stalks look impressive when massed together in a simple arrangement. Here, they have been teamed with golden wheat and dried poppy seed heads in a tin container whose gentle grey tones offset the blues, greens and golds perfectly. If you cannot find an old tin, use any galvanized metal for a similar effect.

MATERIALS
kitchen knife
4 dry florists' foam bricks
tin container, about 23 x 23 x 30cm/
9 x 9 x 12in
2 bunches dried wheat
6 bunches dried lavender
2 bunches dried poppy seed heads
2 handfuls of reindeer moss

1 Fit the florists' foam into the container, using the kitchen knife to trim to size. If you are using a tall container stand two foam bricks upright in the bottom to support the two on top. It is important that the bricks on top fit the container tightly.

2 Insert the wheat, a few stalks at a time, into the centre of the foam. Discard any broken or imperfect stems.

3 Working in rows, insert the lavender stalks one by one around the wheat. Graduate the height of the rows of lavender so that the front ones are slightly lower than the back ones. This gives the impression of a more generous band of lavender.

4 Cut the stalks of the poppy seed heads to about 5cm/2in. Insert a row all around the rim of the container. Place another row behind them so that this row rests on top of the first. Tuck the reindeer moss carefully under the front row, lifting the seed heads a little if necessary.

VERSATILE LAVENDER

Lavender's wonderfully simple, spiky archi-tectural form makes it a natural for making effective indoor decorations, whatever your level of skill. Whether you simply bunch it, or fashion it into a complex tree, the trick is to go with it, rather than try to let it imitate the look of a traditional floral bouquet. Gather it together, stalk and all, straight and soldier-like, into bunches. Alternatively, cut off the stalks and fix the lavender heads into a base for a look that is reminiscent of the fields in full bloom.

LEFT: *This exotic gnarled lavender tree is made up of a driftwood "trunk" secured in a dish of sand, then given a mantle of dried Spanish lavender. If this seems too ambitious, try the mophead trees, or make a Christmas tree version using a cone of florists' foam wedged in a terracotta pot.*

RIGHT: *Bunches of lavender tied around a basket makes for an exquisite, perfumed fruit "bowl". The bunches were first secured with wire, then tied with strips of Provençal-style fabric and knotted to the basket handle with small pieces of blue-dyed raffia. Adapt the idea and make a fragrant indoor decoration by attaching lavender in bunches to the rim of a basket, then filling it with a complementary pot-pourri.*

POTTED LAVENDER

I t is not difficult to make simple lavender arrangements in garden pots for attractive scented displays to last all through the winter. The deep indigo blues look wonderful with bright sunshine yellows, especially when teamed with Provençal-style fabrics to evoke summer days in the south of France. These pots have been colour-washed and then filled with flowers arranged in a neat crop to make the most of the blooms. You could vary the arrangement and make a taller display by building up a fan shape of lavender stems.

MATERIALS
kitchen knife
1 large dry florists' foam cone
terracotta pot, about 15cm/6in tall
10 dried sunflowers
scissors
1 bunch dried lavender
blue-dyed raffia
glue gun and hot glue wax

1 ⤝ Using the knife, cut and shape the florists' foam until it fits tightly into the terracotta pot.

2 ⤝ Cut the sunflower stalks to about 5cm/2in and insert into the foam around the rim of the pot.

3 ⤝ Cut the lavender stalks to about 5cm/2in and insert into the florists' foam to fill the centre of the arrangement.

4 ⤝ Tie several strands of raffia around the pot. Secure in position at the back, using the glue gun and hot glue wax. Trim the ends of the raffia.

FRESH LAVENDER HEART

Little can be more romantic than a fresh
lavender heart. Make one for a special
occasion, then let it dry naturally as an ever-
lasting souvenir. This uses a lot of lavender, so
make sure you have access to plenty before
you begin, or use a smaller wire base.

MATERIALS
To make a heart measuring about
30 x 30cm / 12 x 12in
120 large lavender heads
secateurs or scissors
florists' reel wire or any fine wire
garden wire
florists' tape
green raffia

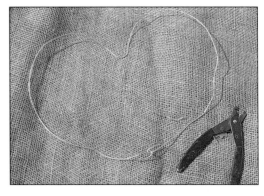

1 ◆ Cut the lavender stems to about
2.5cm / 1in and make up bunches of
about six heads each, firmly securing them
with fine florists' wire.

2 ◆ Make a hook at each end of a piece of
garden wire about 112cm / 44in long.
Link to make a circle, then make a dip at the
top edge and bend into a heart shape.

3 ◆ Using florists' tape, bind the first
bunch of lavender to the bottom of the
wire heart. Place the next bunch a little
further up the wire and bind that on.
Continue until you reach the centre top,
then start again at the bottom and work up.

4 ◆ Make a small bunch of lavender and
secure with wire. Tie with green raffia.
Place at the bottom of the front of the
wreath and bend the stalks to the back. Pass
the raffia to the back to catch the stems and
then secure at the front with a bow.

FRESH TUSSIE MUSSIE

In bygone days, ladies carried herbal tussie mussies as a form of personal perfume. They were usually made of several varieties of fresh herbs arranged in concentric circles. If you are lucky enough to find white lavender, or if you grow it in your garden, it makes up into a delightful tussie mussie when contrasted with the more conventional blue.

MATERIALS
1 bunch blue lavender
1 bunch white lavender
green raffia, similar twine or elastic band
secateurs
ribbon

1 ❧ Arrange a circle of deep blue lavender stems around a small bunch of the white lavender. Secure with a piece of raffia, twine or an elastic band.

2 ❧ Arrange the remaining white lavender around the blue, secure the complete bunch with raffia, twine or an elastic band. Trim the stalks using secateurs.

3 ❧ Complete the arrangement by tying on a wide ribbon, then making a generous, decorative bow.

DRIED LAVENDER WREATHS

Lavender wreaths make for wonderful wall decorations, scenting the room at the same time. Make one pure and simple, or go one step further and decorate the finished wreath with seagrass string and feathers. The basics of wreath-making are the same, this one uses several varieties for added texture.

MATERIALS
3 bunches dried lavender, 2 blue and 1 white
florists' reel wire
wire cutters or scissors
glue gun and hot glue wax
1 willow wreath base, about 20cm/8in diameter
ribbon

1 ⁂ Make up each of the varieties into small bunches and secure them using florists' wire. Make up all the bunches before going on to the next step.

2 ⁂ Using the glue gun, attach the bunches of white lavender in two groups, one on either side of the wreath base, using the bunches to cover the full width of the base. Make a group of another variety of lavender next to each of the sections of the white lavender in the same way.

3 ⊱ Continue with a section of yet another variety, and continue around, alternating the varieties until the whole wreath is covered. Make a ribbon bow to trim. Fix on to the wreath with wire.

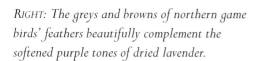

RIGHT: The greys and browns of northern game birds' feathers beautifully complement the softened purple tones of dried lavender.

LAVENDER AND SUNFLOWER GARLAND

Spread a little scented sunshine with a vibrant dried garland. Use it as a celebration decoration, then drape it above shelves, kitchen cupboards or wardrobes to perfume the room decoratively for the rest of the year.

MATERIALS
1 plastic garland case
kitchen knife
4 dry florists' foam bricks
scissors
10 sunflower heads
1 bunch dried curry plant
10 bunches dried lavender

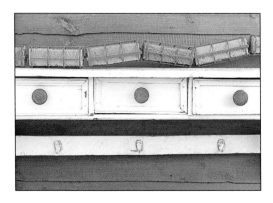

1 ◆ The garland base consists of plastic cases that link together using a hook-and-eye system.

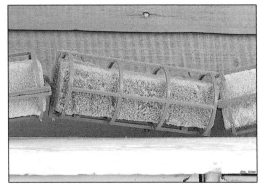

2 ◆ Cut the florists' foam to fit inside the plastic cases, then link them together to make the desired length of garland.

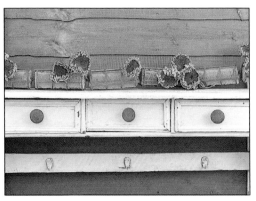

3 ◆ Position the garland on the shelf. Cut the sunflower stems to 5cm/2in. Insert groups of sunflowers at intervals along the length of the garland. Add dried curry flowers around the sunflower heads.

4 ◆ Trim the lavender stalks to 5cm/2in and add them to the garland. Start by working outwards from one group of sunflowers, making sure that whole area of florists' foam is covered before moving to work round the next group of sunflowers.

SWEETHEART WALLHANGING

—⊷⋙⊶—

Create a wallhanging from a heart, roses and lavender – three icons of romance. It is very easy to make, and makes a delightful decoration for any room in the house.

—⊷⋙⊶—

MATERIALS
3 dry florists' foam bricks
heart-shaped copper cake tin, about
30cm/12in across
kitchen knife
paper, pencil and scissors
2 bunches dried roses
4 bunches dried lavender

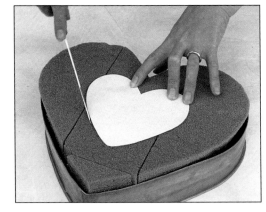

2 ⋙ For the rose centre draw a heart motif onto paper and cut out. Place the heart shape on the foam and draw round with a knife to make a guideline for the roses.

1 ⋙ Line up the florists' foam so it matches the size of the cake tin. Press the cake tin rim on to the foam to make a print of its shape. Using the knife, cut just inside this line so the foam shape will fit tightly into the tin. Use the off-cuts to fill in any spaces.

3 ⋙ Cut the rose stems to 2.5cm/1in. Place a line of them around the rose shape. Here darker roses go round the perimeter and lighter ones in the centre. Finally, add the lavender and fill in, in concentric circles, around the rose heart.

SCENTED NAPKIN RINGS

⚡️

These elegant lavender-filled organza napkin rings, inspired by a hair scrunchy, are extremely easy to make. You could make a few sets, in different colours, to suit a variety of table schemes or celebrations.

— ⚡️ —

MATERIALS

FOR SIX NAPKIN RINGS

0.5m/½yd metal shot organza
scissors
1m/1yd elastic
needle and sewing thread
loose, dried lavender

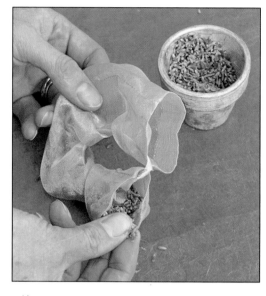

1 ⚡️ For each ring, cut out a piece of organza about 30 x 12.5cm/12 x 5in and a piece of elastic about 12.5cm/5in or the correct length to fit snugly around the napkin. Fold the organza in half lengthways, right sides together. Stitch along the length and turn right side out. Thread the elastic through the organza tube and slip-stitch the ends firmly together.

2 ⚡️ Fill the tube loosely with dried lavender, then slip-stitch the open ends to each other to form a ring of lavender-filled organza.

ABOVE: Tuck a bunch of lavender or any dried flowers or decorative leaves into the napkin ring for added effect.

CHAPTER FIVE

FRAGRANT LAVENDER

THE MOST FAMOUS OF THE NOSE HERBS IS THIS LAVENDER,
WHOSE FLOWER SPIKE, AS MODEST IN HUE AS A QUAKER'S
BONNET, IS HIGHLY FRAGRANT.

L.B. WILDER IN THE FRAGRANT GARDEN

*ABOVE AND LEFT: Fresh or dried, in simple or more elaborate
arrangements, lavender brings a wonderful scent to the home all
the year round.*

Of all lavender's qualities, the most unmistakable is its fragrance. The Ancient Egyptians, Greeks and Romans valued it for its perfume; the Romans used it generously in their celebrated public baths. And since then, for centuries, women have luxuriated in lavender baths, perfumes and cosmetics, besides using it dry to give fragrance to their homes all the year round.

Over the ages, lavender may have enjoyed greater or lesser popularity, but it has never disappeared. Lavender is still a major player in the perfumer's repertoire. Its distinctive aroma which is both sweet and pungent, fresh and slightly medicinal, has a quality that never becomes sickly or cloying. Nowadays, lavender's perfume is associated with women, perhaps because, for most of the twentieth century, it has not been fashionable for men to use perfume. But this was certainly not always the case. The Ancient Egyptian, Greek and Roman men were just as likely to use lavender fragrances as were women. And did they but know, so are today's men!

Lavender is so useful a perfume, long-lasting as it is evocative, that perfumers use it extensively in products for men, too. Even men who do not think they use fragrances, are probably unsuspectingly splashing on lavender

ABOVE: The mere sight of a lavender field in full bloom is enough to evoke its pungent perfume.

in the form of shaving creams and foams, for perfumers use lavender in much the same way as chefs use salt. Even if it is not evident in a fragrance, lavender is very likely to be there, drawing out other aromas.

Lavender water was one of the very first perfumes (as opposed to unguents) to be developed in Europe, made in the twelfth century by a Benedictine abbess, Hildegarde, who wrote prolifically about plants and medicines. But perfume did not become generally used until many years later because the church did not think it seemly to use fragrances. It was not until after Henry VIII dissolved the monasteries that once again the fragrance of lavender became popular. His daughter, Elizabeth I of England, was a great devotee, paying her distillers enough for a single compound to keep them secure for a lifetime.

By Stuart times, the fragrance was being used to scent all kinds of household products such as furniture polish, candles and even soap. It was Henrietta Maria who introduced the Continental idea of perfuming soap and cosmetics to Britain when she married Charles I. It became fashionable for the ladies of large houses to spend hours in their still-rooms distilling lavender oil and using it to concoct lavender waters, creams and potions. They would also dry lavender to use for "sweete bags", and as a base for pot-pourri to scent their rooms.

But the heyday for English lavender came during Queen Victoria's reign. She, too, was very fond of the fragrance, and used to stroll through the lavender fields in Wallington with

her appointed "Purveyor of lavender essence to the Queen", Miss Sarah Sprules, "drinking in" the heady aroma of fresh lavender in full bloom under summer skies. The essence and dried flowers allowed that perfume to permeate her different residences for the rest of the year. Floors and furniture were polished with lavender-scented beeswax, pot-pourri released its aroma into the rooms, lavender water and soaps perfumed the bathroom.

The queen set a fashion for lavender-scented cleaning, washing and polishing products and soon even the most humble abode took on the fragrance of lavender. The trend took root and became a favourite of several generations. But towards the second half of the twentieth century, lavender-perfumed homes became associated with elderly aunts, and its popularity gradually waned.

Lavender is still a favourite fragrance, but lavender gifts and decorations do not have to be rooted in its Victorian heyday. There are many new ways it can be used for making gifts, or as wall or table decorations that look wonderful while releasing that inimitable aroma.

LEFT: Lavender became a popular ingredient for all kinds of cleaning products, valued for its disinfecting qualities as well as its perfume.

LAVENDER PAPER FOLDS

──── ✦❖✦ ────

In the sun-baked markets of Provence, dried lavender is sold in folds of brown paper. It is an idea that can be adapted easily with the help of a colour photocopier to make decorative scented sachets for cupboards, drawers or shelves. You can ask any colour photocopying shop to enlarge or reduce any image to the size you want. Old labels from food packaging were used here but almost any print would be suitable – and, of course, you still have the original intact.

──── ✦❖✦ ────

MATERIALS
A4 sheet tracing paper
soft pencil
scissors
any print for decoration
loose, dried lavender
hole punch
twine

1 ❧ First prepare a tracing paper pattern measuring 20.2 x 28.5cm/8 x 11¼in. Draw a straight line parallel to one long side, 2.5cm/1in in from the edge. Draw another line parallel to this 11cm/4¼in from the same edge. Draw a line between these two lines 8.5cm/3¼in from the top, and another the same distance from the bottom. This panel shows the space and positioning for the photocopied image. Take this tracing and the print to a colour photocopying shop and ask them to enlarge or reduce the image to fit the panel, printing this more or less in the middle of an A3 sheet. Position the tracing over the photocopy so the image is in the right position. Draw around the tracing, then cut out along these lines.

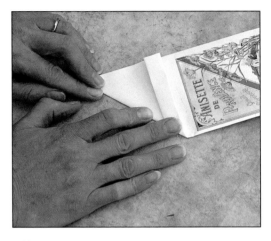

2 ❧ Make the first fold along the inside edge of the image so the paper is folded almost in half. Crease and unfold. Turn the paper over, face down on a smooth surface, and fold down along the position of the line close to the long edge. Crease and unfold. Re-fold the first fold, then fold one long edge over the other so its edge meets the second fold line. Fold both thicknesses of paper in the position of the second fold. This provides a seal along the whole length of the sachet. Turn the sachet over and at one end, fold down the corner so the folded seal comes to the front.

3 ✠ Fold the top point down so it tucks into the folded seal. Fill the sachet with dried lavender from the open end.

4 ✠ Fold the open end in the same way as before. Use a hole punch to make a hole in the corner, and attach twine.

HOUSEHOLD LAVENDER

The still-rooms of old, presided over by the mistress of the house, were where polishes, soaps, perfumes and dyes were made as well as where foods were preserved and medicines formulated. Richly aromatic lavender would have had a leading role to play for many of these functions. Furniture polish may have been made from beeswax and lavender; candles would have been scented with lavender; lavender would have been hung up in bunches to dry in the still-room. Oil would have been distilled, pot-pourris mixed and stalks of the lavender preserved to throw on the fire to give fragrance to the living-rooms. In later years, it may have been the butler who presided over furniture polishes, candles and fire sticks. Today people are equally familiar with the scent of lavender in household products: soaps, polishes and all manner of cleaning materials, even spray air-fresheners. Much of the lavender perfume used in modern household products comes from the thriving lavender industry in Spain.

LEFT: *Save the dried stems of lavender, bundle them up and throw them on the fire for a natural aromatic room scent.*

RIGHT: *Dried lavender is a traditional ingredient for scenting furniture polish, candles, soap and a wide range of cleaning materials.*

ORGANZA CUSHION

—⊱✦⊰—

D ried lavender flowers seen through translucent organza, contribute to the design of this exquisite cushion. They provide a delightful pale indigo texture while releasing their fragrance to scent the whole room. The backing is in linen, which adds weight and gives the whole cushion a wonderful feel.

—⊱✦⊰—

MATERIALS
scissors
0.5m / ½yd purple linen
0.5m / ½yd purple metal shot organza
pins, needle and sewing thread
1 large bag dried lavender
1.25m / 1½yd wide ribbon
1m / 1½yd narrow ribbon
4 gold tassels (optional)

1 ⊱ Cut out a 30cm / 12in square in linen and a matching one in organza. With wrong sides together, turn in the edges all round. Pin and tack. Stitch through all the layers, leaving a 10cm / 4in gap for filling. Measure the combined widths of the ribbons and use pins to mark this amount in from each side of the cushion. Use the pins as guides to the correct distance from the edge for stitching, leaving a gap corresponding with the gap in the first row of stitching for filling.

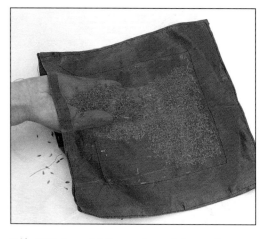

2 ⊱ Fill the middle section of the cushion with lavender. Stitch to close. Stitch along the outside edge to neaten.

3 ⊱ Cut two lengths of the wide ribbon to the length of the width of the cushion. Fold down the corner of each and crease. Trim to near the crease-line.

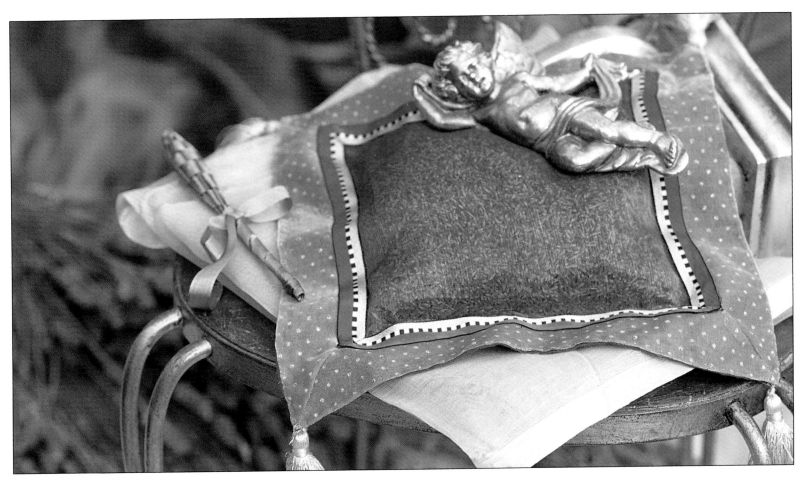

4 Using small running stitches, hand-stitch along the diagonal close to the edge. Repeat on all four corners.

5 Hand-stitch the outside edge of ribbon to the outside edge of the cushion, then stitch the inside edge of the ribbon in place.

6 Repeat the same operation with the narrow ribbon. Hand-stitch the tassels to the corners at the back of the cushion.

LAVENDER POMANDER

This delightful lavender version of a spice pomander makes an aromatic room decoration any time of the year or an imaginative Christmas tree decoration.

MATERIALS
medium-gauge florists' stub wire or
garden wire about 40cm/16in long
1 dry florists' foam ball, about
9cm/3½in diameter
45cm/18in ribbon
wire cutters
2 bunches dried lavender
scissors

1 Bend the wire in half and fix through the centre of the ball. Pass the ribbon through the top loop and push down so that it is fixed firmly to the ball. Trim the ends of the wires. Bend the wires at the bottom flat against the foam to secure the ribbon.

2 Select similar-size lavender heads, and, starting at the bottom of the ball, push the stalks into the foam, making a circle around the circumference of the ball.

3 When the first circle is complete, make another circle of lavender around the circumference at right angles to the first. This will divide the pomander into quarters.

4 Working in lines, fill in one quarter. Repeat with the others. Tie a bow at the top of the ribbon.

LAVENDER CANDLE RINGS

The Scandinavians have a great tradition for making candle rings from all sorts of materials to decorate the tops of candlesticks. These lavender ones make a very pretty table decoration, while adding to the ambience with their exquisite aroma. Make sure you snuff out the candles before they are low enough to burn the decorative lavender and candle rings.

MATERIALS
medium-gauge garden wire
wire cutters
1 bunch dried lavender
scissors
fine-gauge florists' wire
narrow satin ribbon

1 ⋡ Make a ring of garden wire that will easily slip over the candle, but which is snug enough to rest on the top of the candlestick. If you do not have any garden wire, make a ring using several thicknesses of florists' wire, then use another piece to twist around the ring tightly to hold all the

thicknesses together. Make small bunches of lavender and trim the stems to about 1cm/½in. Secure the bunches with fine florists' wire if necessary.

2 ⋡ Bind the bunches of lavender to the ring using fine florists' wire. Thread the ribbon through the wire ring at the front, then tie in a bow to finish.

LAVENDER OIL LAMPS

⊢◆⊱⌶⌶⊰◆⊣

O il lamps make an original alternative to candles as a table decoration. They look wonderful grouped into an arrangement, some stood on glass stands to create a variation in heights. By scenting shop-bought blue candle paraffin with a few drops of lavender oil, it is easy to create a romantic and aromatic lamp light for the room.

1 Using the small funnel supplied with the oil lamps, pour in some blue lamp oil to a depth of about 2.5cm/1in.

2 Drop in about ten drops of lavender oil, then wash through with a little more lamp oil. Be careful not to over fill the lamp.

Do not leave the lamps burning unattended and keep out of reach of children.

RIBBON HANGING

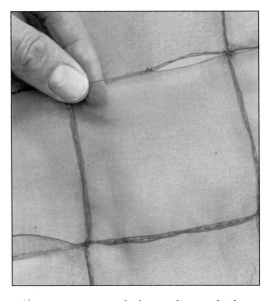

This exquisite gossamer wallhanging is made from two shades of chiffon ribbon, woven together, then scented by tiny bouquets of lavender tucked into the pockets created by the weaving. This hanging is not difficult to make, but as the ribbon is very slippery, it is fiddly and needs patience.

MATERIALS
6.5m / 7yd chiffon ribbon in another toning
colour, 7.5cm / 3in wide.
5.5m / 6yd chiffon ribbon in one colour,
7.5cm / 3in wide
scissors
pins, needle and sewing thread
paper and pencil
1 bunch lavender
1m / 1yd narrow purple rayon ribbon
1m / 1yd narrow pink rayon ribbon
narrow copper piping

1 ✄ In main colour ribbon, cut four lengths measuring 1m / 1yd 3in and four lengths measuring 60cm / 2ft. In toning colour, cut three more long and four short lengths. At one end of each of the longer lengths, fold a double hem to make a casing. Slip-stitch. Lay these longer ribbons on a flat surface next to each other, alternating the colours, with the casing at the top, wrong side down. Weave one of the short lengths through the longer lengths, aligning the top edge with the casing. Make several small neat stitches at the corners where the ribbons cross. Weave through another short ribbon in the toning colour and stitch. Continue with the remaining ribbons.

2 ✄ Next, top-stitch the pockets, which not only hold the bunches of lavender, but give the hanging a quilted effect. Start by "quilting" all the verticals. Let the sides of the vertical ribbons overlap very slightly, then make tiny running stitches along the overlap. You will find you are stitching through three layers: two verticals and a horizontal. The horizontals are stitched in a similar way, except where the horizontal ribbon is at the front of the hanging, you will need to leave the tops open to make the pockets. At these points, make the running stitches just through two layers – the vertical ribbon and the horizontal one running behind it.

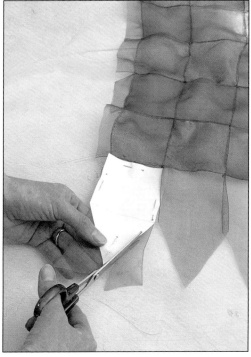

3 ❧ Cut the ends of the vertical ribbons into points. The most accurate way to do this is to first make a paper template, pin this to each ribbon in turn and cut out. Trim the horizontal ribbons so they are of an even length.

4 ❧ Make bunches of three stems of small-headed lavender and tie each one with purple or pink rayon ribbon. Tuck them into the pockets. Thread the copper piping through the casing and hang on metal hooks.

POT-POURRI IN A GAUZY BAG

Gather dried lavender heads into an exquisite pompon of metal shot organza, tied with wide velvet ribbon in a generous bow. It looks wonderful, smells wonderful and, unlike most other pot-pourris, it does not collect dust.

MATERIALS
1m/1yd purple metal shot organza
scissors
needle and sewing thread
3m/3¼yd narrow rayon ribbon
dried lavender heads
1m/1yd broad velvet ribbon

1 ✦ Cut one piece of 40cm/16in organza and four 40 x 10cm/16 x 4in strips for the facings. With right sides together, sew a strip on opposite sides of the square. Sew the other strips to the other two sides of the square. Trim the seams, snip off the corners and turn the facings to the wrong side.

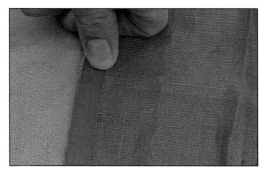

2 ✦ Top-stitch all around the edge of the square. Use the rayon ribbon to neaten the edges of the facings: cut a length of ribbon a little longer than the side of the square, turn the ends in, then stitch in place over the raw edge of the facing. Repeat on all four sides.

3 ✦ For each corner tassel cut four lengths of rayon ribbon about 12.5cm/5in long, fold in half and stitch another small piece of ribbon in place near the fold. Trim the ends at an angle. Stitch to the corner.

4 ✦ Spread out the finished organza square, facing side upwards. Place a handful of lavender heads in the centre, then gather up all four corners to make a pouch and tie with a flamboyant bow.

LAVENDER WATER

1 Put 350g/12oz/3 cups of lavender and 600ml/1 pint/2½ cups still mineral water into a pan and bring slowly to the boil, stirring constantly.

2 Simmer for ten minutes, remove from the heat and allow to cool. Strain into a bottle and add 150ml/¼ pint/⅔ cup of vodka. Shake well.

RIGHT: Lavender sweet water has been a favourite since the twelfth century. Splash it on for a refreshing fragrance, or add it to footbaths to soothe the feet at the end of a hot day.

LAVENDER AND BATHING

Lavender and bathing have gone hand in hand since Ancient Egyptian times. Treat yourself by adding a few drops of lavender oil to the bath water to lift spirits and ease aching muscles. When you get out of the bath, splash on refreshing lavender water.

ABOVE: Lavender-scented bath crystals, oils and cosmetics make wonderful aromatic and healing treats after long, stressful days.

LAVENDER SOAP

1 ✿ Infuse ten lavender flowers in 60ml/4 tbsp/¼ cup boiling water for 30 minutes. Strain.

2 ✿ Grate plain soap into the infusion over a low heat and stir constantly until thoroughly mixed.

3 ✿ Press the mixture into balls and allow to dry and harden. This will take at least two days. There are plenty of other lavender gifts that are easy to make, even if you do not have a lot of time to spare – the secret is in beautifully presenting bought lotions, soaps and creams.

RIGHT: You may not have the time or inclination to make your own lavender soap, but you can still put together a charming lavender bath gift by wrapping lavender soap attractively, tying it with string and sealing with wax, then teaming it with toning lavender sachets in natural linen.

BATH BAG

Hang a lavender-filled linen pocket over the hot running tap and you will have a relaxing, naturally scented bath.

MATERIALS
pencil and paper
scissors
0.5m/½yd natural linen
pins, needle and sewing thread
button, 2.5cm/1in diameter
coloured string for hanging

1 ⚘ Make a paper pattern template. Cut out one complete shape in linen. Cut a rectangle the same width as the pattern but 16.5cm/6½in long for the front of the pocket. Use the pointed end of the pattern to cut a facing that measures 15cm/6in.

2 ⚘ Stitch a narrow hem at the top of the pocket's front and the bottom of the facing. With wrong sides facing, pin the front and facing to the back of the pocket and stitch all around. Trim the seams, snip the corners and the top point. Turn right side out and top-stitch all round. Make a button hole in the point of the flap and sew on the button. Fasten the button, then make a handle by passing a piece of string under the flap at the top and tying in a knot.

BATH SCRUB MITT

Let the healing properties of lavender oil get to work after a hot summer's day outside when grasses, burrs and brambles have made their mark on hands and legs. Lather up the outside of this mitt with soap as normal, then tuck a lavender-filled sachet into the heart-shaped pocket. As you scrub, the lavender is crushed and releases its oils.

MATERIALS
tracing paper
pencil and paper
scissors
honeycomb or terry towelling flannel
in navy blue
honeycomb or terry towelling flannel
in lime green
pins, needle and sewing thread
fuchsia-coloured stranded embroidery thread
0.5m/½yd coloured muslin
dried lavender

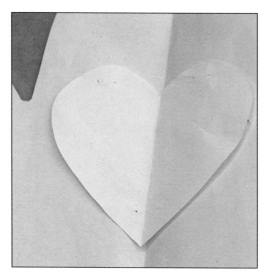

1 Make a paper pattern by tracing the glove and heart templates. Cut out in paper. Cut any borders off the flannels. Cut two hand shapes from the navy blue flannel and one heart shape from the lime green.

2 Turn in the edges of the heart shape and stitch all round. Make a hem at the bottom edge of both of the hand pieces. If you are right-handed, place one hand piece right side upwards with the thumb facing to the right. If you are left-handed, place the thumb facing towards the left. Lay the heart centrally on the hand, pin at the widest points. Stitch the edge of the lower half of the heart to the mitt between the pins.

3 Using two strands of embroidery thread, work blanket stitch around the edge of the heart so that the solid line covers the original stitching. Stitch through all the thicknesses where the heart is joined to the mitt, and just through the heart thickness at the top where it is free. This provides strength to the heart.

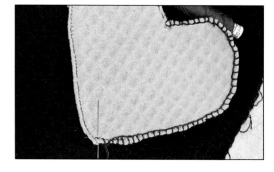

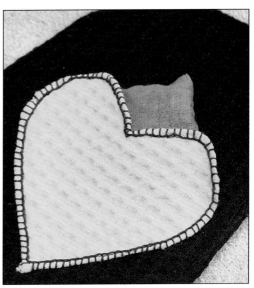

4 ⚜ With right sides facing, stitch the two mitt pieces together. Snip into the seam allowance at the curves and turn right side out. Top-stitch around the mitt. Stitch together 5cm/2in coloured muslin squares along three sides to make sachets and fill with dried lavender. Turn in the top edge of each one and stitch to close. Throw away the sachets after they have been used.

LAVENDER TO GIVE

A gift of lavender, however simple, is always welcome. If you don't have time to make something from scratch you can buy a gift and present it in an original way.

LEFT: These miniature painted picture frames have added appeal when each is given a tiny bunch of dried lavender.

BELOW: Turn dried lavender into a special gift by presenting it in a cone of cellophane tied around with a generous amount of satin ribbon.

ABOVE: An embroidered lavender bag and matching cushion make a delightful gift when presented in a toning wooden basket.

RIGHT: Pretty white cotton handkerchiefs filled with lavender and tied with gossamer ribbons make for the simplest, yet most charming of lavender bags.

LAVENDER OVEN GLOVE

Fill an oven glove with lavender so that you will smell its fragrance every time you pick up a warm pot or plate.

MATERIALS
1m/1yd ticking
scissors
scraps of scrim, muslin or cotton
0.5m/½yd wadding
pins, needles and sewing thread
dried lavender

1 ✄ Cut two pieces of ticking 75 x 20cm/ 30 x 8in wide. Round off the ends. Then cut out six rounded pocket ends 20cm/8in long; two in ticking, two in scrim and two in wadding.

2 ✄ Cut the remaining ticking into bias strips 4.5cm/1¾ wide. Make a double hem along the straight edge of the ticking pocket ends.

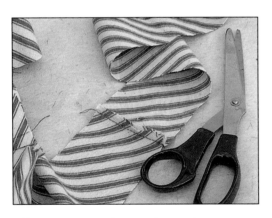

3 ✄ Stitch a wadding pocket and a scrim one together. Fill with lavender. Stitch closed. Stitch the bias together to go round the glove; use a short piece for a loop. Fold a 7cm/2¾in length of bias in half length-ways, wrong sides together, and stitch.

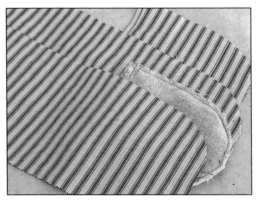

4 ✄ Assemble the oven glove. Lay one ticking pocket end right side down, lay a full length piece right side down on top of that, then the lavender-filled wadding sachet and the other full length piece right side up.

5 ✄ Pin the bias around the oven glove, right sides together. Pin the loop in position halfway down the mitt, with the loop tucked inside and the raw edges level with the raw edges of the bias and main piece. Stitch all around.

6 Trim close to the seam, and cut into the seam allowance around the curves. Turn the bias around to the other side of the oven glove. Turn in the edge and stitch again to finish off.

CHAPTER SIX

DELICIOUS LAVENDER

THE YOUNG AND TENDER SPROUTINGS ARE KEPT IN
PICKLE AND RESERVED TO BE EATED WITH MEAT, AS
DIOSCORIDES TEACHETH.

THE HERBALL, JOHN GERARD, 1597

ABOVE: Old-fashioned crystallized lavender, sweet and fragrant.
LEFT: In centuries past, lavender's aromatic qualities made it a
popular flavouring. Nowadays it is not so commonly used, but it
can turn an ordinary dish into something
much more exotic.

Of all the aromatic herbs, lavender must be the most pungent, yet, in modern times, it has been largely ignored in the kitchen. It is hard to understand why – rosemary has a similar sweetly aromatic quality, yet it has earned a place in some of our most traditional dishes.

In the past, lavender has had an important role in the kitchen. Elizabeth I was particularly partial to lavender conserve, and in her time, it was not unusual for lavender to be used in savoury dishes too. One reason for lavender's popularity as a flavouring in those days, it has to be said, was to disguise the taste of meat that was past its best.

The use of lavender, along with other fancy tastes, probably went out of fashion when the Puritans imposed a simple diet, a trend that was not reversed until relatively recently when foreign travel introduced exotic flavours to the western world.

With the new appreciation of perfumed flavours, perhaps lavender could be reinstated into mainstream cooking. As far as savoury dishes are concerned, lavender can easily be substituted for rosemary to lend an exotic flavour to a simple dish. Try it with lamb or fish; in salads, savoury tarts and savoury breads. However, traditionally, lavender is used more

ABOVE: Lavender can be used either fresh or dried as an aromatic culinary herb.

often in sweet, rather than savoury, dishes.

One of the easiest ways to impart its aromatic flavour to cakes, biscuits, sweets and desserts, is by making lavender sugar, to use instead of ordinary sugar in the mixtures. If you do not enjoy baking, sprinkle lavender sugar over summer fruits or puddings for

added piquancy. As well as being used as a flavouring, lavender flowers make decorative garnishes. Either use them fresh, or crystallize them, just as you may crystallize violets, to decorate summer sponge cakes or exotic after-dinner chocolates.

As the spike can be fairly woody, it is inclined to be rather crunchy, and not at all palatable, so use whole flower spikes for decoration only where they can be removed before eating – on the tops of cakes or puddings, for example, or even to decorate the rims of plates and platters. Where the flowers are going to be eaten, take each floret off the stem, pinch the bottom ends out and use to sprinkle over, or even mix into, salads and desserts. The varieties with the deepest indigo shades are the most effective. Choose fully opened flowers from each spike, not only because they are the prettiest, but because these are the ones that will be most flavoursome.

When using fresh flowers, make sure you do not pick any that may have been contaminated with pesticides, bearing in mind that winds can carry sprays – so check with near neighbours. It is best not to wash the flowers as they are easily spoilt, so choose the ones that appear the cleanest. There should really be no need to clean them anyway since

ABOVE: Lavender sugar, used to sprinkle over fruits or in making jams and preserves, brings an old-world charm to tea-time.

lavender grows high off the ground and most insects and birds avoid it. The only fleeting visitors are bees and butterflies. Pick the flowers in the morning when the dew has dried but the sun has not had time to dissipate the oils. If they are still damp, let them dry out away from direct sunlight as that is inclined to make the flowers open and release their precious oils. Any dampness left on the flowers will soon spoil them, making them wilt and, in time, become mildewed. If you are using dried lavender, ensure you buy culinary quality which has been specially grown and packaged under hygienic conditions.

CRYSTALLIZED LAVENDER

This perfumed decorative garnish for sweets and puddings makes a refreshing alternative to crystallized violets. It is best to take the individual lavender florets off the rather unpalatable stalks. You can do this before or after you crystallize them, depending on the variety. While well-spaced florets are easy to remove after crystallizing, you may find it easier to remove the florets of the more tightly-packed varieties, such as "Hidcote" before crystallizing them.

Take the top stalks of fresh lavender and remove each floret. Discard the stalks, then, using tweezers if necessary, dip each floret first into lightly whisked egg white and then into caster sugar. Leave to dry on layers of greaseproof paper. When they are completely dried out, you can store them between layers of greaseproof paper in an airtight container for up to three months.

LAVENDER SUGAR

⊶⊶✦⊷⊷

This perfumed sugar lends an exotic aromatic flavour to any sweet recipe. Make up several jars in the summer, then package them in attractive glass containers tied around with ribbon for gifts.

⊶⊶✦⊷⊷

INGREDIENTS
15ml / 1 tbsp dried culinary lavender
1kg / 2¼lb / 4½ cups caster sugar

Mix the lavender and sugar together thoroughly and store in an airtight container for at least a month. Shake well regularly. Use for making cakes, puddings and summer drinks, sifting the lavender flowers out before use.

LEAFY LAVENDER SALAD

It is not only lavender flowers that impart fragrance and flavour – the leaves do too. In common with many herbs, they have a naturally slightly hairy texture, so chop them thoroughly before use. Any lavender leaf turns a green salad into something very special – if you have access to the pretty fern-like ones, so much the better.

INGREDIENTS
115g/4oz/2 cups mixed green lettuce leaves, such as lollo biondo, rocket, iceberg, round lettuce and lamb's lettuce
5ml/1 tsp dried lavender leaves, roughly chopped
45ml/3 tbsp sunflower oil
15ml/1 tbsp white wine vinegar
salt and ground black pepper

Wash and prepare the salad leaves. Place the lavender leaves, oil, vinegar and seasonings in a screw-top jar and shake until well emulsified. Toss the dressing over the salad leaves and serve.

RED MULLET WITH LAVENDER

Cook up a barbecue with a difference by adding lavender to fresh mullet for a delicious aromatic flavour. Sprinkle some lavender flowers on the coals too. Eaten alfresco, this will be a memorable meal with a delightful perfumed ambience.

INGREDIENTS
4 red mullet, scaled, gutted and cleaned
45ml/3 tbsp fresh lavender leaves or 15ml/1 tbsp dried lavender leaves, roughly chopped
salt and ground black pepper
roughly chopped rind of 1 lemon
4 spring onions, roughly chopped

Marinate the mullet in the remaining ingredients for a at least three hours. Drain off the marinade, removing the lemon rind. Cook on a very hot barbecue for five to seven minutes on both sides. Brush on extra marinade as it cooks. The fish can also be fried or grilled.

LAVENDER HEART BISCUITS

In folklore, lavender has always been linked with love, as has food, so make some heart-shaped biscuits and serve them on Valentine's Day, or on any other romantic anniversary.

INGREDIENTS
115g/4oz/½ cup unsalted butter, softened
50g/2oz/¼ cup caster sugar
175g/6oz/1½ cups plain flour
30ml/2 tbsp fresh lavender florets or 15ml/
1 tbsp dried culinary lavender, roughly chopped
25g/1oz/2 tbsp caster sugar, for sprinkling

MAKES 16–18

1 Cream the butter and sugar together until fluffy. Stir in the flour and lavender and bring the mixture together in a soft ball. Cover and chill for 15 minutes.

2 Set the oven at 200°C/400°F/Gas 6. Roll out the mixture on a lightly floured surface and stamp out about 18 biscuits, using a 5cm/2in heart-shaped cutter. Place on a heavy baking sheet and bake for about ten minutes until golden.

3 Leave the biscuits to stand for five minutes to firm up then, using a palette knife, transfer them carefully from the baking sheet on to a wire rack to cool completely. You can store the biscuits in an airtight container for up to one week.

FENNEL AND LAVENDER TARTS

Fragrant lavender combines perfectly with the aromatic flavour of fennel. These unusual and mouth-watering tartlets make an appealing summer starter.

INGREDIENTS
FOR THE PASTRY
115g/4oz/1 cup plain flour
pinch of salt
50g/2oz/¼ cup chilled butter, cut into cubes
10ml/2 tsp cold water

FOR THE FILLING
75g/3oz/6 tbsp butter
1 large Spanish onion, finely sliced
1 fennel bulb, trimmed and sliced
30ml/2 tbsp fresh lavender florets or
15ml/1tbsp dried culinary lavender,
roughly chopped
150ml/¼ pint/1 cup crème fraîche
2 egg yolks

SERVES 4

1 ❧ Sift the flour and salt together. Rub the butter into the flour until the mixture resembles breadcrumbs. Stir in the water and bring the dough together to form a ball. Roll out on a lightly floured surface to line four 7.5cm/3in round, loose-based flan tins. Prick the bases with a fork and chill. Preheat the oven to 200°C/400°F/Gas 6. Melt the butter in a pan and add the onion, fennel and lavender. Reduce the heat to low. Cover with wet greaseproof paper and cook gently for 15 minutes until golden.

2 ❧ Line the pastry cases with greaseproof paper and bake blind for five minutes. Remove the paper and bake for a further four minutes. Reduce the oven temperature to 180°C/350°F/Gas 4. Mix the egg yolks, crème fraîche and seasoning together. Spoon the onion mixture into the pastry cases. Spoon the crème fraîche mixture on top and bake for 10–15 minutes until the mixture has set and the filling is puffed up and golden. Sprinkle a little extra lavender on top and serve warm or cold.

LAVENDER CAKE

Bake a summer-scented cake that is reminiscent of those distant Elizabethan times when lavender was extremely popular not just for its fragrance but for its distinctive flavour, too.

INGREDIENTS

175g/6oz/¾ cup unsalted butter, softened
175g/6oz/¾ cup caster sugar
3 eggs, lightly beaten
175g/6oz/1½ cups self-raising flour, sifted
30ml/1 tbsp fresh lavender florets or 15ml/1 tbsp dried culinary lavender, roughly chopped
2.5ml/½ tsp vanilla essence
30ml/2 tbsp milk
50g/2oz/½ cup icing sugar, sifted
2.5ml/½ tsp water
a few fresh lavender florets

1 ❧ Preheat the oven to 180°C/350°F/ Gas Mark 4. Lightly grease and flour a ring tin or a deep 20-cm/8-in round, loose-based cake tin. Cream the butter and sugar together thoroughly until light and fluffy. Add the egg gradually, beating thoroughly between each addition, until the mixture becomes thick and glossy. Fold in the flour, lavender, vanilla essence and milk.

2 ❧ Spoon the mixture into the tin and bake for one hour. Leave to stand for five minutes, then turn out on to a wire rack to cool. Mix the icing sugar with the water until smooth. Pour over the cake and decorate with fresh lavender florets.

LAVENDER SCONES

L end an unusual but delicious lavender perfume to your scones – its fragrance marries well with the sweetness of summer soft fruit and makes for an elegant, romantic tea-time treat. Nowadays, the flavour can seem quite surprising, because the scented quality of the lavender permeates through the well-known tea scone.

INGREDIENTS
225g / 8oz / 2 cups plain flour
15ml / 1 tbsp baking powder
50g / 2oz / butter
50g / 2oz / sugar
10ml / 2 tsp fresh lavender florets or 5ml / 1 tsp dried culinary lavender, roughly chopped
about 150ml / ¼ pint / ⅔ cup milk

1 Set the oven at 220°C/425°F/Gas Mark 7. Then thoroughly sift the flour and baking powder together. Rub the butter into the flour mixture until it resembles breadcrumbs. Stir in the sugar and lavender, reserving a pinch to sprinkle on the top of the scones before baking them. Add enough milk to make a soft, sticky dough. Bind the dough together and then turn it out on to a well-floured surface.

2 Shape the dough into a round, gently patting down the top to give a 2.5cm/1in depth. Using a floured cutter, stamp out 12 scones. Place on a baking sheet. Brush the tops with a little milk and sprinkle over the reserved lavender. Bake for 10–12 minutes until golden. Serve warm with plum jam and clotted cream.

TEMPLATES

LEFT: Sweetheart Wallhanging.

RIGHT: Shaker Sachet; enlarge to 17.5 cm (7 in) high.

BELOW: Bath Bag; enlarge to 14 cm (5½ in) x 20 cm (8 in), with an extra 12 cm (4½ in) for the point.

TEMPLATES

To enlarge the templates, use either a grid system or a photocopier. For the grid system, trace the template and draw a grid of evenly spaced squares over the tracing. To scale up, draw a larger grid onto another piece of paper. Copy the outline onto the second grid by taking each square individually and drawing the relevant part of the outline in the larger square. Draw over the lines to make sure they are continuous.

ABOVE: Ribbon Hanging pointed ribbon ends; should measure 7.5 cm (3 in) square, with extra for the pointed end.

LEFT AND RIGHT: Bath Scrub Mitt; enlarge the mitt to 16.5 cm (6½ in) by 26 cm (10 in).

USEFUL ADDRESSES

UNITED KINGDOM

Cameron-Shaw, 279 New King's Road, London SW6 4RD. Tel: 0171-371 8175. Dried arrangements with flair.

Damask, Broxholme House, New King's Road, London SW6 4AA. Tel: 0171-731 3553. Linens, cushions, lavender bags, bath treats.

Norfolk Lavender, Caley Mill, Heacham, King's Lynn, Norfolk PE31 7JE. Tel: 01485 570384. Lavender plants, dried lavender, distiller of pure lavender oil and seller of lavender products.

V. V. Rouleaux, 10 Symons Street, London SW3. Tel: 0171 730 3125 A wonderful range of ribbons.

Something Special, 263-265 London Road, Mitcham, Surrey CR4 3NH. Tel: 0181-687 0128. Wholesalers of florist's supplies who will mail order in small quantities too.

Wallace Antiques, High Street, Cuckfield, West Sussex RH17 5SX. Tel: 01444 415006. Wonderful antique furniture and accessories for home and garden.

AUSTRALIA

The Australian Lavender Growers' Assoc., RMB E1215, Ballarat, Vic 3352 Ph: (053) 689 453 Fax: (053) 689 175

Carol White
Lavandula Lavender Farm
Main Rd, Shepherds Flat, Hepburn Springs Vic 3461 Ph: (054) 764 393
Plants, display gardens, lavender products

Yuulong Lavender Estate,
Yendon Rd, Mt Egerton, Vic 3352.
Ph: (053) 689 453 Fax: (053) 689 175
Lavender grower, plant sales (fresh & dried), lavender products (craft, culinary and cosmetic). National Registered Collection of Lavenders (more than 80 different lavenders).

Tanja Lavender,
811 Bermagui Rd, Tanja, NSW 2250
Ph: (064) 940 159
Lavender grower, distiller of lavender oil, lavender products.

Monaro Country Lavender,
P.O. Box 236, Bombala NSW 2632
Ph: (064) 587 203
Co-operative of lavender growers.

Di's Delightful Plants
P.O. Box 567, Lilydale Vic 3140
Ph: (03) 9735 3831
Lavender plants by mail order.

Bridestowe Estate Pty Ltd
RSD 1597, Nabowla, Tas 7254
Ph: (003) 528 182
Lavender farm, large distiller of lavender oil, retail outlet stocking oils, dried flowers and gift lines.

Orton Australia
R.M.B. 4004A, Talgarno, Vic 3691
Ph: (060) 201 136 Fax: (060) 201 186
Suppliers of fresh and dried bunches of lavender, seed for pot pourri, essential oil (10ml bottles).

USA

Herb Shoppe
215 W. Main St
Greenwood, IN 46142
(317) 889-4395
Suppliers of bulk herbs, pot pourri supplies, essential oils, herbs and others.

Gailann's Floral Catalog
821 W.Atlantic St.
Branson, MO 65616
Offers a full line of floral supplies and dried flowers.

San Francisco Herb Co
250 14th st.
San Francisco, CA 94103
Offers a full line of herbs including lavender.

Tom Thumb Workshops
PO Box 357
Mappsville VA 32407
(804) 824-3507
Suppliers of dried flowers, containers, ribbons, floral items, spices, herbs and essential oils.

INDEX

ACKNOWLEDGEMENTS

No book is the work of just one person: it is always the result of the energy and enthusiasm of a whole team. My very special thanks go to Debbie Patterson for her inspiration and the sheer artistry of her glorious photographs; to Joanne Rippin for her wit and humour, for having the vision to steer this herb into fresh fields and the flexibility to let the ideas mature; to Liz Trigg for her delicious recipes; to Ann and Henry Head of Norfolk Lavender for their support and astounding energy, for supplying the most superb lavender to work with, and for checking the technicalities; to Tony Hill of Wallace Antiques for his fabulous location; to Damask for lending me wonderful lavender bags and accessories; to Cameron-Shaw for lending the evocative lavender tree on page 68 plus several containers; to Gloria Nicol, who kindly contributed the lavender candle rings from her Candle Book, and particularly to Nigel Partridge for the outstanding and elegant design of this book.